ALL HILLS HIGH AND LOW

Walking the Herriot Way

Paul Amess

Kingston House Publishing

CONTENTS

WALKING THE HERRIOT WAY

Introduction

I f you are reading this book, which you certainly seem to be, then the chances are that you have probably heard of James Herriot and quite possibly the footpath that bears his name. For anyone that has not heard of him, it's not your fault, so come along anyway, but very briefly, James Herriot was the vet that became famous through *All Creatures Great and Small*, and all will be explained as we walk the route that bears his name. That aside, I think it is fair to say that the Herriot Way is probably the best short, long-distance footpath in the world, if you know what I mean, and that is no exaggeration. Come with me, then, on this amazing voyage of discovery.

Starting in Aysgarth, in the heart of beautiful Wensleydale, the path follows a 52-mile circular route through some of the most beautiful countryside imaginable. Our journey initially proceeds west, through Askrigg and towards Hawes, before turning north over Great Shunner Fell, the third highest mountain in Yorkshire, and up to Keld, before another right turn heads east, through Swaledale and towards Reeth. A final southerly section brings a possibly now tired, smelly and quite probably blistered walker back to Aysgarth where all the fun originally began, but on the way, you would have taken in high fells and heather-clad moors as well as beautiful market towns, traditional Yorkshire villages, and a whole lot more besides.

Wensleydale, by the way, is one of the few dales not named after its river, unlike Swaledale, Wharfdale and many other dales that dot this beautiful part of the north of England, an area which is collectively known, not surprisingly, as the Yorkshire Dales, although technically only the upper, more northern dales are classed as being in the Yorkshire Dales. Wensleydale, then, is instead named after the village of Wensley, at the far eastern end of the dale, and is one of the places where the delicious, crumbly cheese that bears its name was originally made.

This now small village used to be much more important, but over the centuries became something of a backwater, particularly after being decimated by the plague in 1563. Nowadays, the village is not known for much at all, it has to be said, although there are a couple of things worth mentioning.

Firstly, it is the final resting place of a doctor called Peter Goldsmith. Never heard of him? Well, Goldsmith was the surgeon on board HMS Victory at the Battle of Trafalgar on 21st October 1805, and he was thus by the side of none other than Admiral Horatio Nelson when he popped his clogs. Just because Nelson died, however, doesn't make Goldsmith in any way a bad doctor, as Nelson had sprung a rather large leak thanks to a sneaky French sniper and was already well on his way to shuffling off this mortal coil.

Secondly, Wensley has a very fine church. Holy Trinity was built in the 1300s, and while it is very pretty to look at, it is also the church where James Herriot was married in the original television series of *All Creatures Great and Small*.

Anyway, even though the dale is not named after its river, which, as we have heard, is the custom of so many other dales, there is still a river running through Wensleydale, and that would be the River Ure. How you pronounce Ure is debatable, but I am told by local people that they prefer to pronounce it the same way as you would say *Your*. It was previously recorded as the River Jor way back in the 1100s, and it later became known as the River Yore. Yoredale, then, is the old name for Wensleydale.

The walk, then, is based on one taken by the well-known country vet and writer James Herriot, real name Alf White, or James Alfred Wight in full, although for reasons of clarity, I shall generally refer to him solely by his pen name of James Herriot within these pages. The name change came about because the Royal College of Veterinary Surgeons prohibited vets from undertaking any form of advertising, and it is said that he chose Herriot as his new moniker after seeing Scottish international footballer Jim Herriot playing rather well for Birmingham City F.C. in a televised game.

Anyway, he took this walk with his son Jimmy, turning it into an actual walking holiday and staying at Youth Hostels in Aysgarth, Keld and Grinton along the way. While you can still stay at the hostel in Grinton, Aysgarth has since closed, and the one at Keld is now a pub and hotel called Keld Lodge, and although it is supposed to be very nice, expect to pay an appropriate price if you decide to follow Herriot's itinerary word for word.

It is probably important to mention that the route Herriot took is not actually the same as the one followed by the official footpath that bears his name today. He actually set off from Leyburn, and after spending his first night as mentioned in Aysgarth, he went straight to Keld, spending Saturday night there with Sunday night spent in Grinton. The official walk adds Hawes to this itinerary but completely misses out Leyburn, which also means that Wensley is skipped too. This is odd because Herriot spoke of Leyburn fondly, saying that it held *a thousand happy associations* for him, while he does not appear to have been so fond of Hawes. In his book *James Herriot's Yorkshire*, which is basically a guide to all of his favourite places, he fails to mention Hawes at all. Why the official path differs so much from the one he took is a mystery, but nonetheless, it is still said to be a fantastic walk anyway.

James Herriot, then, had been born in Sunderland, County Durham, in 1916. However, his family soon moved to Glasgow, where he spent much of his childhood and, by the time he left home, he certainly considered himself a Scot. After graduating from veterinary college, he moved to Yorkshire in 1940 and initially believed there was no scenery outside Scotland. He soon changed his mind, however, and it is well known that he lived the rest of his life in Yorkshire doing exactly what he loved best, which was taking care of animals of almost every kind and encountering many interesting adventures along the way.

However, what is not well known is that he also did a brief stint working back in his birthplace of Sunderland. This job, though, was reliant upon a greyhound stadium, and it was partly due to the unpredictable nature of this work that he soon found himself in beautiful Yorkshire. And thank goodness he did, otherwise, we would not have his wonderful stories to entertain us today. Eventually, he put pen to paper and wrote about these adventures and his various encounters with both animals and people and, not surprisingly, his books became bestsellers, one after another.

Herriot was particularly influenced by his initial employer and life-long mentor, Donald Sinclair. An unconventional character at best, Herriot renamed Sinclair in his books as Siegfried Farnon, but what is perhaps most surprising for anyone that has read Herriot's books or seen any of the television series is that the portrayal of Sinclair was actually toned down compared to the real-life man, who was in fact really somewhat eccentric. For instance, it is said that Sinclair once fired off a shotgun at a dinner party purely and simply to not so subtly suggest to his guests that it was time to buzz off and go home. Furthermore, actor Samuel West, who thoroughly researched Sinclair's character for the latest television series, denied that the man was eccentric. Instead, he said this would actually be something of an understatement and went on to describe him as being *as mad as a box of frogs*.

This eccentricity was also portrayed excellently by none other than Sir Anthony Hopkins in the original 1977 movie version of *All Creatures Great and Small*. Coming across as a socially clumsy but ultimately lovable human being, Hopkin's portrayal of Sinclair was said by many to have hit the nail on the head.

Herriot's descriptions of Sinclair did, perhaps understandably, put something of a strain on their relationship; however, Sinclair being the luvvie that he was, eventually overcame these difficulties, and the pair carried on working together for many years to come. Herriot generally did try to change the names of the people and places depicted within his books, partly to avoid this exact problem, so his wife Joan became a fictional Helen. He also created the imaginary town of Darrowby, where Herriot set much of his work, which was, in his own words, a bit of Thirsk and something of Leyburn, Middleham and Richmond, as well as a fair amount of his own imagination thrown in for good measure.

Finally, Herriot also admitted that around half of the content of his books was just complete fiction, which only serves to make it better in my eyes. One notable point, for instance, is that Herriot's career actually began during the dark days of the Second World War, but he instead chose to set his stories in the idealized setting of the 1930s, which further helped to make it difficult for people to identify the true identities of his fictional characters. This is further reinforced, of course, by the fact that he set his stories here in the heart of the Yorkshire Dales, while as we have already heard, the real surgery was up in Thirsk, though you couldn't have chosen a better setting, to be honest.

Alas, Herriot was diagnosed with prostate cancer in 1991, after which he received treatment for many years. Sadly, he passed away on 23rd February 1995, aged 78, at his beloved family home. He did, however, leave an impressive legacy that still lives on to this day, with his books going on to become popular films and television programs that are still being remade as we speak and which remain as popular as ever, if not more so.

While he was alive, though, Herriot never took to fame, and it is fair to say that he remained down to earth right up until the day he died. He was not particularly driven by money, either, and continued to live a relatively modest life, with his only luxury, if it can be called that, being his purchase of a house in 1977 in a more remote location, notably in the village of Thirlby near Thirsk, which was purely intended to help retain whatever privacy he could for his family following his worldwide fame.

The walk, then, has become more and more popular partly down to the television series, but also because people are increasingly turning to the great outdoors and the beautiful English countryside. Indeed, people travel from all over the world to follow the route almost as a pilgrimage to James Herriot himself, with ever-increasing numbers of people completing the walk with each passing year.

This year, I have decided to become one of those pilgrims too. My reasons for doing it are mixed. I like the television program, enjoy walking, and absolutely love animals. However, the main reason, if truth be told, is that I've put on rather a lot of weight recently. I did join a gym, and indeed, I was there just yesterday. I was trying out the new machine they had installed, but I had to stop after around 30 minutes as I felt slightly ill. It was excellent, though, and it did Mars Bars, Kit Kats, Double Deckers, and a whole lot more besides.

On a serious note, I am also bringing my faithful dog Belle along with me on this wonderful journey. She's getting a bit old now and deserves an adventure, in my mind anyway, but my kids were somewhat concerned when I first suggested taking her on a 52-mile walkies. She has been out with me many times over the last few weeks, though, as part of a sort of training regime, and it is probably worth pointing out that it is, in fact, always me that is the one struggling to get back home and never her, which is clearly a good sign, for her at least.

We acquired Belle from our neighbours when she was just 6-months old. They were a nice couple who had bought her as a puppy but had unfortunately divorced, and not wanting to leave her home alone all day while at work, had appealed for new owners. We had jumped straight in, as we had always been a dog family and had sadly just lost our previous dog of many years, a wonderful cross named Beauty, a few months before.

Beauty died on 23rd December, which is Christmas Eve Eve when you think about it, and although there is never a good time to lose your much-loved pet, this time of year seemed particularly cruel. My children were still pretty young then, so they were terribly upset by her passing. Rather funnily, they expressed clear disgust when a puppy failed to materialize on Christmas Morning just a couple of days later.

Belle, then, was instantly welcomed into the family, and although we still don't know exactly what type of dog she is, being something of a Heinz 57, she certainly has the look of a Labrador Retriever. Within hours of her coming to live with us, the kids were taking turns to ride her around the house as if she was a horse, and she instantly became an important, perhaps the most important, member of our family.

My youngest son immediately took great delight in telling us some amazing facts about dogs that he had looked up, including that a dog's sense of smell is forty times better than a human's and that the average dog is as intelligent as a two-year-old, although they are obviously somewhat easier to train. I mean, have you ever tried to train a two-year-old child to fetch a ball or a stick, or even just to stay still? It's impossible, and anyway, the other people in the park got upset when I tried this with my son, but that might be because he wasn't on his lead and wasn't wearing his muzzle.

Back on a more serious note, dogs can also sniff at the same time as breathing and can be either left or right-handed (well, pawed), and you can find out which your dog is quite easily. Simply throw them their favourite toy or a ball, and see which paw they use to get it. Belle is a lefty, but it took us a long time to find this out as, being a bit stupid, she kept using her mouth every time we did the test.

The first months of her living with us can only be described as colourful. We already had a cat, a rather mature and somewhat miserable tortoise-shell called Otto, who mainly enjoyed eating and sleeping as her chief hobbies. She wasn't too keen on the new puppy that continually bounded clumsily around the house, which was rather unfortunate, as the puppy was actually quite keen on Otto and wanted to constantly play with and chase her no matter what time of the day or night it happened to be.

On more than one occasion, then, Belle came to me with bits of cat claw sticking out of her nose, which must have done the trick, as she eventually learned to keep away from the deranged moggy, if not all of the time, then at least some of the time.

Belle was also fond of chewing things, as puppies tend to be, and despite buying her a nice juicy rubber toy in the shape of a bone as well as her own teddy bear, which lasted less than a day, it should be noted, she still chewed her way through our dining table and chairs, our skirting boards, and on one particularly noisy night when the neighbours chose to let off lots of fireworks, even our dining room door.

I got my revenge, though. When she was still very young and thus rather small, she was sniffing around the chair I was sitting in looking for some dropped treats. I had been watching a film and stuffing various savoury snacks down my gizzard, and Belle had already figured out that I was not the world's tidiest eater.

What I did not realize, however, was that our new little puppy had then snuggled in a little ball at my feet and had gone to sleep, so when I decided to operate my chair, which was a sprung recliner, I inadvertently flung poor Belle straight across the room like some kind of missile. She must have woken up mid-flight and wondered what the hell was going on, and all would probably have been well and good if she had not then landed on that grumpy cat, which had been quietly asleep for several days on the small bean bag at the other side of the room. Of course, the cat immediately woke up, shrieked out in alarm and promptly deposited several more claws into poor Belle's nose. All in all, it was actually very funny, but my wife was not amused, and the cat ignored me for a fortnight.

Anyway, somehow managing to survive our crazy house, she finally grew out of chewing anything and everything that she could get into her mouth, but not until she was around 5-years old, though we still have the table and chairs as evidence, just in case.

And now that she is fully grown, Belle can run for many miles and often has. There is a disused railway line near where I live, and when she was still fairly young, one of her earliest trips was down this track all the way to Hornsea on the East Yorkshire coast.

She got there without a problem and still had plenty of energy, but there was one thing I didn't realize about Belle, and that was the fact that she is a bit stupid. Don't take this the wrong way, as she is very much loved by us all, but there is no getting away from the fact that she is a bit dim and often behaves like a two-year-old, so maybe my youngest was right after all. In fact, come to think of it, Belle is probably more like a one-year-old.

It took ages for her to learn how to fetch something, and as I said, many cat claws became stuck in her nose before she realized that it might, just might, be a very good idea to keep away from the furry thing that lived on the couch and which had razor blades attached to every limb.

Anyway, in Hornsea, Belle inevitably discovered the beach, and although I had given her lots of drinking water along the way, it turned out that Belle just loved water of any kind and dived straight into the sea. She then played a game of biting the water by constantly attacking it. She must have drunk quite a bit of this salty brine, as a strange and unfortunate incident occurred about thirty minutes later.

Her tail went up, and something rather watery and unpleasant started coming out of her. Unfortunately, we were by then on the nice little high street that could be found in the centre of Hornsea, and for a while, I did not realize what was going on.

I only found out when I stopped to tie Belle to a fence while going into a shop. I noticed that her tail was up, and she had left a rather interesting trail for the last few hundred yards, much to the disgust of various old ladies who were now tutting rather loudly and glaring in my direction.

This wasn't something you could possibly pick up, and while being stared at by several angry blue-rinse-toting pensioners, I made a feeble attempt to clean up the mess with a bottle of water, though this just made matters worse and simply served to spread the unpleasantness further across the path.

This continued on much of our journey back, which was some miles, it has to be said, but it thankfully stopped just a mile or two from home. Unfortunately, Belle also stopped, somewhat exhausted and dehydrated from her wretched experience, and I had no option other than to ring my wife, who then drove to pick up our very tired little doggy.

The latest unfortunate incident happened just a few weeks ago when I had popped into our local shop for a newspaper. I tied Belle up to a small bin next to an ice-cream van and went inside to grab my paper, but when I came out, Belle was gone, and so was the bin. I followed a trail of rubbish that led behind the shop and into the park, where I found Belle running around in circles on the grass and occasionally glancing behind her, clearly terrified of the big black thing that was apparently chasing her round and round. Bits of rubbish, mainly ice-cream wrappers and empty drinks cans, were bouncing out of the bin and leaving a considerable mess, which is when I noticed the park ranger glaring angrily in my direction. He was perhaps not entirely pleased, as up until our unfortunate visit, he had been doing a bit of a litter pick in the park, but all of his work had now been well and truly undone.

When I finally managed to grab Belle, and after returning the bin to the ice-cream van, I spent quite some time collecting rubbish under the watchful eye of the park ranger, and we have never been back since.

Anyway, walking the Herriot Way is the plan, and with Belle for company, what could possibly go wrong?

LONGER THAN EXPECTED

Aysgarth to Hawes (nearly)

Leaves fell all around me as autumn turned slowly into winter, and it was to be on one of the last mild days of the year when Belle and I began our walk of the Herriot Way, although I obviously did not know this at the time.

The drive to Hawes took a little under three hours, and as we pulled up into the centre of this bustling but tiny village, I realized that this was probably the longest car journey that my faithful dog had ever been on.

She had behaved impeccably and had spent almost all of the aforementioned three hours snoring and drooling on the back seat, probably dreaming of chasing little kitties.

Luckily, I was in my wife's car, so I was not overly concerned about the doggy drool and, more importantly, the countless hairs that she would probably leave behind, because this particular canine is a notorious shedder.

As I have already mentioned, Belle is some kind of Labrador cross, or at least we think she is. She sheds hair like no tomorrow, and I have personally witnessed her wandering around the house, leaving a fine trail of her golden fleece right before my eyes. In fact, it is sometimes possible to follow this trail to find out wherever in the house she happens to be snoring on any given day, and we have even had to buy one of those special vacuum cleaners that claim to do the job when it comes to animal fluff.

I sometimes wonder why she hasn't gone completely bald, as considering what she leaves behind her every day, it is somewhat astonishing that there is any hair left on her at all, yet somehow her thick coat remains as persistent as ever. My hairline, in stark contrast, is receding as rapidly as a greyhound, or perhaps at the same speed as Usain Bolt, just to give you some idea, though for some unfathomable reason, I hardly ever have to hoover my own sheddings from the floor.

Anyway, as we already know, the Herriot Way traditionally starts in Aysgarth, or so I am told. This is exactly where we will be starting today, so you may be wondering why on earth we have just arrived in Hawes. Well, normally, I am accompanied on these little adventures by my fellow foolish friends Rob and Chris, but today Chris was required at work to change a light bulb or something, and Rob is suffering from a deadly bout of man flu. I had also asked my dad if he fancied a wander through some boggy fields in the rain, but he had suddenly remembered that he had an optician's appointment or a flat tyre or his leg had fallen off, or something along those lines anyway.

I got the impression, then, that nobody wanted to come on this particular adventure, which is when my gaze settled upon the dog. I think I know when the exact moment was that she realized she was coming on a very long walkies with me, as her ears dropped at the same time as she made a high-pitched whining sound and curled up in a little ball on the sofa, with her eyes now firmly averting my gaze.

At first, she refused to budge, as although I said it was mild, it was still very early in the morning when we set off, and therefore quite dark and cold outside at this ridiculous and unearthly hour. To be honest, any sensible person, dog, or any other sentient being at all come to think of it, would probably take one look outside and go back upstairs to bed until, oh, I don't know, the end of March perhaps, given the frozen northern latitude that we live at.

Anyway, I had finally managed to persuade her to jump into the car with a meaty nibble or two. She soon settled on the blanket that I had placed for her on the back seat, and as I said already, this is where she lay perfectly well behaved and making unusual doggy snoring and farting noises for the next few hours. As I drove along, I wondered whether or not a dog's superior sense of smell made her farts smell forty times worse because some of hers were bad as it was. And by the way, Belle is in good company when it comes to bottom-burps. Did you know that Pumbaa was the first character to fart in a Disney movie? Amaze your friends with this fact, because not many people know that. And if you think it's a pointless fact, you'll thank me when that question comes up during a quiz.

However, the truly important fact to get from all this is that there was only one human being among our little walking group today, which meant there was only one driving licence. Normally on these walks, we would take two cars and leave one at the end of the walk. However, as Belle's driving ability was probably somewhere down there with that of a neanderthal, I was effectively going solo in this regard. The plan then was to leave the car in Hawes, somehow get to Aysgarth by other means, and then walk back to the car. Simples.

Only it wasn't. I had checked the bus timetables, which appeared to be different depending upon which source you used, and had even fired off an email to the bus company. Helpfully, they managed to send me back exactly the same timetable that I already had, which was one of the most confusing I had ever seen, although it was incredibly colourful.

The timetable helpfully told readers that some services ran only on Darlington College Days, whatever they were, and obviously, as I had no idea when the college days were, this was of little use to Belle and me. Other colour codes suggested that you had to ring the driver on his mobile phone in order to get a pick-up from certain locations, and yet other services were demand-responsive, and you had to book these three years in advance, apparently. Unfortunately, as well as not knowing whether or not Darlington College was open on any given day, I had been unable to really plan this trip, and just to top it off, I am also colour blind, so there you go. This timetable was, therefore, useless to me.

I had, perhaps somewhat recklessly, decided instead to just turn up and see if there was a bus on the day, and if not, we would just wander around Hawes for a few hours and think of something to do, and maybe try to walk whichever bit of the trail was hereabouts. Imagine how surprised I was, then, when the bus turned up at exactly the right time and in exactly the right place. I must remember to buy a lottery ticket, I thought to myself, while I was on this run of extraordinarily good luck.

When I say bus, though, it was not what us city types expect of a bus, but it was really just a big van with windows and seats. I nearly broke it, too, when I tried to pull the handle to open the door, but luckily, I just managed to hear the driver shout something at me, *idiot* perhaps, followed by a click and a hiss, after which a star-trek type door magically opened right before my eyes.

Belle, who had been sat patiently licking herself somewhere quite impolite, took one look at the bus and decided that no, she was not getting on that, thank you very much, which meant that I would have to do all the donkey work. I carefully picked her up, deposited her in the van, and then climbed up the steep steps too. She had put on a fair bit of weight, I thought to myself, but who am I to talk?

She was shaking just a little bit, possibly because she had never been on a bus of any kind before, but after paying the driver, I settled into my seat, and she snuggled into my legs for the next stage of our little trip.

I imagined she was having some kind of sensory overload today, what with constant new smells and new sights bombarding her, but at the same time, she also seemed to be enjoying herself somewhat.

As the little bus trundled off, Belle snuggled further into my legs so as not to wobble and fall around as we gained speed along what were rather bendy roads, and luckily, there was not a lot of legroom, which was good for her as she was wedged in nice and tight, but not so good for me, as I could not move due to having been crammed in like a sardine by an overweight pooch.

There were only two other people on the bus, and I suddenly realized that I had stupidly managed to sit myself directly next to them for some unknown reason. Now I am not sure about you, but whenever I have found myself on an empty bus, and someone sits down next to me, I immediately panic. I assume them to be some kind of nutter, perhaps recently escaped from an approved institution, or possibly even worse.

Luckily, these two were very nice and turned out to be called Neil and Val. They were local, they said, and were on their way to Leyburn to do their weekly shop. They asked me if we were out walking, which must have been pretty obvious, to be honest, and although I was tempted to tell them we were going scuba diving in Malham Tarn, just to see what their reaction would be, I said that yes, we were indeed out for a walk and, specifically, we intended to start the Herriot Way today.

I had hoped that they were then going to tell me that they had done it themselves and go on to regale me with stories of all of the adventures that they had encountered along the way, but alas, they did not but instead told me that they had never done that one, which was a bit of a let-down to tell you the truth.

The conversation naturally died off, but Val did keep reaching across to stroke Belle, who had now managed to somehow roll over in her cramped and confined space, and was busy enjoying the occasional belly rub as a reward.

I enjoyed the view out of the window, which was a classic Yorkshire view of hills, forests and, of course, dry stone walls, and I had to occasionally grab hold of the chair in front of me as the bus was flung around blind corners at quite an impressive speed, it has to be said.

The roads became narrower to the point that you began to think they would actually stop at any second, but they somehow went on, and I am almost positive that we drove through a farmyard and across a field at one point, which was simultaneously both quite a surprise and somewhat exciting, it has to be said.

Anyway, after half an hour or so, the bus pulled up next to the village green in Aysgarth after passing a beautiful old house on the corner, which was Heather Cottage. Belle was much keener to get off than she had been to get on, moving off as soon as that door opened, and she initially navigated the steps down pretty well. Unfortunately, she took a misstep on the last one and tumbled onto the tarmac below, but she did manage to do a rather impressive body roll before getting up and looking around to see if anyone had been watching. I think she was more embarrassed than anything.

Anyway, beautiful Aysgarth stands in the Richmondshire district of North Yorkshire, a wholly beautiful area in itself, and I am afraid we are just going to have to get used to using such words as beautiful, outstanding and picturesque, as this whole area is simply an abundance of nature at its very best.

Even the towns are incredibly nice to look at, with many fine old buildings built of old Yorkshire stone in a traditional and pleasing manner that never becomes old, if you get what I mean.

This particular village is perhaps best known for its waterfalls, quite aptly called Aysgarth Falls, that lie just to the north. The River Ure flows west to east here, and it is near the village where it cascades over a series of low waterfalls over a distance of about a mile or so. The waterfalls are actually a set of three falls and are well worth a visit, and as well as featuring in the works of famous artists such as Ruskin and Turner and even William Wordsworth, they most recently and perhaps somewhat more famously popped up in the movie *Robin Hood Prince of Thieves.* In the movie, we can witness Kevin Costner being repeatedly tossed over the upper falls by a rather violent Little John before Costner gets right back up and gives John the whipping he deserves, which culminated in him getting a thwack somewhere rather painful indeed.

Turner's visit to the falls probably did not involve hitting anyone in the crown jewels and was presumably a much more sedate affair. Joseph Mallord William Turner, usually just called William Turner, visited these falls on 28th July 1816 and simply painted the beauty that he saw. In a scene that has changed little to this day, his painting is instantly recognizable for what it is and is one of many paintings that he did in and around Yorkshire at the time.

While it would be easy to imagine Turner as one of your typical upper-class painters of yesteryear, this is far from the truth. He grew up in London and retained his east-end Cockney accent throughout his life. He was often troubled and was forced to accept commissions just to get by, and when he came up to Yorkshire to paint the countryside, this was one of the best-paying jobs he had ever had. He remained troubled, though, and like Herriot's mentor Donald Sinclair, many described Turner as eccentric. There is even a reliable account of him sailing a boat into the middle of the Thames on the night of the census just so he wouldn't have to put down an address. Subsequently, he never really attained any great wealth. In fact, he lived in poverty and suffered poor health in his later years before dying from cholera in 1851, aged 76. He painted pretty good pictures, though, which are worth an absolute fortune nowadays, including the one of Aysgarth Falls.

We took a minute to get our bearings, and while I sat on a bench and checked the map, Belle wandered around and marked everything with her scent, which I thought was a bit rude, to be honest. I mean, if I went somewhere, and the first thing I did was the same as what she had just done, people would be up in arms.

The map suggested that we head north, through a gap in some houses, and down a small path that should eventually lead us to the river. There was no sign or any other indication that this was the start of the Herriot Way, not that I could see at least, and while I had not really given this much thought, lots of other long-distance paths do have something to mark where the start is. Hadrian's Wall Walk springs to mind in this regard and has splendid start and finish points that are very hard to miss, but that is officially classed as a national trail, whereas the Herriot Way is not, so that could have something to do with it.

Leaving pretty Aysgarth behind then, a small snicket led us in between some pretty stone cottages, and with that, we were off. I let Belle off her lead, which she loved, darting ahead of me, but her freedom was short-lived, as rounding a corner into a field, we were met with a battalion of sheep. There were dozens of them, all merrily bleating away and grazing on the lush green grass that covered the meadow, but they soon shut up when they saw the pair of us. If you have ever seen one of those movies where a stranger walks into a bar, and all of the locals stop what they are doing and just stare, it was a bit like that, only none of the sheep were drinking whisky, and I think most of them were unarmed. Anyway, it was both funny and fascinating, and the sight of dozens and dozens of sheep transfixed on a single point is not one I had seen before.

Belle's ears stood on end, and she stared intently at the strange snacks before her, not quite knowing what to make of them. She had seen sheep before, of course, but the farmers near us generally grow crops, so it had only been the odd one or two that she had come across before, and certainly not the huge flock that stood before her now, staring her down as they were.

I was quite relieved and somewhat impressed when she didn't slip from my grip and go on a murderous rampage, as a dog is just a cultivated wolf, of course, and they do still occasionally feel the same instincts to chase meaty little feasts such as sheep, cats and squirrels. Indeed, Belle did have one such episode a couple of years ago when she suddenly took off after something, leaving me huffing and puffing and trying to catch her up. When I finally found her behind a tree and up against a fence, she was licking and presumably washing a somewhat terrified looking cat that did not quite know what to make of its new best friend. On another occasion, she managed to have an unfortunate encounter with a rather large hedgehog. I imagine she would never make that mistake again, as her tongue had swelled to twice its usual size shortly after.

We wandered through the flock, now heading firmly downhill and towards a farm, all under the beady eyes of these fluffy oddities, and Belle was looking warily left and right, still not quite knowing what to make of them all.

The farm was Aysgarth Mill, and although there was nobody around, it certainly appeared to be a working farm, with various bits of unidentified machinery lying around, much of which was a puzzle to me, although I did recognize a log splitter.

Heading west, the path now took us along the banks of the River Ure, and although there were one or two small waterfalls, the main waterfalls which Aysgarth is famous for were around a mile or so downstream to the east, which meant they were behind us, and we would not see them until we completed more or less the whole of the Herriot Way, which would certainly not be today.

Soon enough, the river gave way to fields, where we found ourselves in a very pretty meadow, although it was a bit boggy, with the sheep seeming to be sinking.

A man called Christopher Booth grew up in these very fields, although it is actually Sir Christopher Booth, and while you may never have heard of him, he was very big when it came to, well, poop. Human poop, to be exact. Booth grew up in Wensleydale and was Yorkshire through and through. Although he often lived away from here, he always kept a cottage in Wensleydale and would often return for holidays where he would enjoy fish-ing on this very river. He became quite famous, in the medical world at least, for discovering all sorts of interesting things about vitamin B12. However, whoever defined interesting in this sense does not perhaps quite understand the meaning of the word, as none of it is interesting enough for me to include within these precious pages, I am afraid.

He was a lot more than a doctor, though, starting his career during the dark days of the Second World War as a diver. He spent most of his days blowing things up and sending them to the bottom of the sea, and also learned to speak several languages during his postings, presumably including such handy phrases as *put your hands up, drop it or I'll shoot,* and *oh look what a nice fish.* Incidentally, these phrases continue to be useful on nights out in Leeds to this very day, particularly that last one. He then went on to study medicine, which is much more creative than blowing things up, of course, and is something that then became his life's work. He also wrote several biographies, though how he found the time is hard to imagine for such a busy man.

These biographies were mainly of prominent figures in the medical community, including William Hillary, Robert Willan and John Haygarth, all of whom we will actually encounter later on this little walk of ours, as well as a book about a man called John Fothergill, a dales doctor and close friend of Benjamin Franklin, one of the founding fathers of the United States. How a dales doctor managed to befriend one of the most powerful men in the world, though, I have not been able to fathom, but anyway, more of him later.

The best bit about Christopher Booth, though, is what I am going to tell you next. He was always an ardent left-wing proponent when it came to politics, and while he was working at Hammersmith Hospital, where the atmosphere was decidedly also left-wing, he was once heard telling someone exactly where he would shove any offer of a knighthood, which was somewhere dark and dank. He certainly seems to have changed his mind at some point and certainly by 1983, which is when they awarded him one, and which is something that he certainly does not appear to have shoved anywhere, dark, dank or otherwise.

And finally, the cherry on the cake of this little story is as follows, and although I'm sorry that it took so long to get here, it really is worth it. During the turbulent 1980s, when unions were demanding pay rises, bottles of milk, and free kittens for all, one of his doctor colleagues suggested that taking a demand for a pay rise to Margaret Thatcher would be like *raising a red rag to a bull*. After just a second of contemplation and in his usual dry style, Booth soon corrected this statement, though, and said that it would actually be like *raising a red rag to an old cow*. Wherever you stand with your politics, it is hard not to see the funny side in old Christopher Booth.

Today, these meadows were pleasantly devoid of sheep, so Belle was once again off her lead and running crazily around, clearly having more fun than you could shake a stick at, with yet more new sights, sounds, and smells to keep her entertained. Unfortunately, when I turned around, intending to shout to her to catch me up, I realized Belle was somehow a different colour. Rather than her usual golden colour, she now took on the hue of something like a chocolate Labrador, and after a split second of processing, it dawned on me that she had been rolling in something rather smelly.

We have already heard that a dog's sense of smell is many times greater than that of a human, but I think it is only right to quantify this further at this stage. When my son told me that a dog's sense of smell is around forty times better than that of a human, what this actually means is that the area of the brain that processes doggy sniffs, the olfactory bulb, is forty times larger than ours, on average. Therefore, this actually means that a dog's sense of smell is many thousands of times more sensitive than ours, with breeds such as Bloodhounds and German Shepherds not surprisingly at the top of the smelly list, if you get what I mean. Furthermore, the olfactory recess, which is the part of the dog's nasal cavity that houses the receptors that pick the smells up in the first place, is also many times larger than the human equivalent. And finally, if you have ever wondered why your dog's nose is always wet, it is to enable him or her to more easily absorb scent chemicals.

All of this, then, is the amazing result of millions of years of evolution and is what allows modern dogs to do amazing things such as sniff out explosives, save the lives of avalanche victims, and discover sausages hidden in bushes. Furthermore, they can detect illnesses such as diabetes and cancer at extremely early stages, which is surely pretty helpful, along with many more medical conditions, and this is partly because cancerous cells release different metabolic waste products compared to healthy cells. Your precious beast can even let you know you are pregnant well before you have taken a test, so beware when your little fluffball next comes to cuddle up.

And what is Belle using her amazing biological superpowers for today? I'll tell you what she is using them for. She is using them to find and roll around in sheep shit.

I stood there, staring at her, not really comprehending that she was absolutely covered from head to toe in sloppy brown poop. I was probably in denial but soon came back to my senses and did the only thing I could under the circumstances. I texted my wife and told her that her car would probably need cleaning at the weekend, helpfully remembering to include a little smiley emoji at the end along with a couple of kisses, confident that I had just made her day. I'm an awesome husband, I thought to myself.

There would be no point in cleaning Belle now, though, and I reasoned that her covering would probably not do her any harm either, at which point I saw her mouth open and her head reach down to a rather large lump of nastiness. You can probably imagine what happened next. I never actually witnessed it myself, to be honest, as my self-preservation instincts kicked in, closing my eyes and forcing me to turn and flee.

We plodded on, and a few moments later, I managed to witness exactly what Belle had been doing to make herself so dirty. Every few steps, she seemed to throw herself at the ground and slide along, either on her sides, belly or back, which instantly explained how she had managed to change colour so quickly and so effectively. It was actually quite an impressive manoeuvre that she was making, and I reasoned that not many dogs could manage such antics, which probably explains why you don't see that many dogs wandering around totally covered in poop.

The path took us out of the fields and along a short stretch of road, but only for a few yards, after which we found ourselves back in a meadow and heading for a bridge where we would cross the river. We had been on the southern bank of it for the last half-mile or so, but after we crossed, we would spend almost all of the rest of the day on the northern bank until we would cross it once more on our walk down into Hawes. Most of the first half of the walk would be more or less flat as we generally followed the course of the river, according to the map anyway, with a slightly hillier section after Askrigg, but for now, the only hills were firmly in the distance.

Unfortunately, deep in thought, I had not realized that the field we were crossing did not have a gate at the other side. I walked up and down just to double-check, but this only confirmed what I already knew. A high fence, topped with barbed wire, meant we were going no further this way.

With Belle back on her lead, there was only one option: to crawl under a tiny gap in a piece of wire fence back onto the road. It looked as if dozens of hikers before me had made the same mistake, and the gap was certainly big enough, but it was very low down, and I imagined I would get a bit muddy. It was either that or walk back a few hundred yards, though, which did not seem to be a very attractive option, so I let the dog get through first and, still holding onto her lead, did my best limbo impression, and slid under. On a positive note, I pondered, at least I would be more of a colour-match with Belle.

I think it was my rucksack that caused the problem, as I felt something snag which pulled me just enough to make me lose my balance. To cut a long story short, my bum ended up in a rather deep puddle. I sighed and picked myself up and noted, with some irony, that parts of me really were now the same colour as my little chubby dog.

It was only a short hop along the road to the bridge over the River Ure, which was narrow and clearly just for pedestrians, and I had wondered if Belle would be a bit apprehensive about crossing it, but when I let her off her lead again, she was off like a rocket.

At the other side, she instinctively went towards the water, but I shouted her back, concerned that the current may be a bit strong in a river of this size, which was to say a fairly wide one.

I was still a bit apprehensive about letting her off her lead, especially with all of the hazards of the countryside around us, though I was particularly concerned about the water, as Belle loved the stuff of course, and presumably mistook herself for a duck every now and then, and not a dog.

My mind suddenly recalled the first time we ever let her off her lead, which had turned out to be an absolute disaster, though it had not involved water. We had been in the middle of a rather large area of thin woodland and presumed we had the place to ourselves. Belle was quite happily going in and out of the bushes and around the trees as we walked along, but then something awful happened.

We rounded a small clump of trees into a clearing and came across a young family having a picnic on the ground. For some reason, they were all panicking and had their arms flailing in the air, and then I realized why. Belle was already there with them and was taking a rather keen and incredibly active part in their picnic.

She'd already bounced onto their blanket and stolen a sandwich from their young child, and as I ran towards her calling for her to stop, she stuck her head in their hamper and promptly helped herself to whatever had been inside. If the ground had opened up, I would happily have jumped in right there and then; it was awful. But what made it even worse, if that was possible, was that my own kids were laughing their heads off at our mischievous little puppy. It was quite a while before I dared let her off that lead again, I can tell you.

Anyway, she darted among the bushes and the hedges, sniffing out new smells and having a whale of a time, and thankfully never dived into the river, though after a few hundred yards, more sheep appeared, so she once again found herself firmly attached to me.

I mentioned that Belle had never seen so many sheep together, and it dawned on me that I don't think I had ever seen so many either. They were everywhere, and each seemed to be a different shade, with some spotlessly clean while others were clearly filthy devils. Maybe they were world-class rollers, too, just like Belle. There was also the occasional black one, and get this, several were bright red. I don't just mean a subtle shade of ginger, but I mean full on letterbox red through and through. I can only presume that a farmer had painted them so as to identify ownership, as I doubt a rural Banksy is going around the dales tagging livestock, but you never know. Banksy, in case you didn't know, is a guerrilla-style graffiti artist, often said to be from Bristol.

Belle once again enjoyed the odd roll in something dubious, but I resigned myself to the fact that the damage was already done, and no matter what she did now, there was no way she could make herself any dirtier. With that, she found something better than sheep poop, which was a giant cowpat.

Looking as if it had been deposited quite recently, it measured about 18-inches across and at least six inches deep. Crusty on the outside perhaps, I was pretty sure that the inside would not be the same, and as Belle rapidly approached it, I was powerless to intervene. Repeated shouts of her name did nothing, and my final *don't you dare* was equally ignored. I had visions of my wife's car in an absolutely unspeakable state and also foresaw my own premature funeral. However, at the last moment, something inside Belle's head told her that it was probably not a good idea to stick her head into this particular splodge after all, and she veered off to sniff some nettles instead. I released the breath that I did not know I had been holding and immediately realized I could breathe again.

I considered putting her back on her lead but figured that as she was having such a good time out here, a lead would be tantamount to torture for her. Furthermore, knowing Belle's love of water, I figured it was only a matter of time before she would get a good soaking anyway, which would wash off at least the worst of her new coat. I only put her back on the lead when we came across yet more sheep.

We were still walking along the riverbank, which was dotted with trees and bushes, and were a couple of hundred yards south of what appeared to be the line of the old Wensleydale Railway. Suddenly, I felt a tugging on my right arm and immediately realized that Belle wanted to go for a bit of a run and was apparently not too concerned about whether or not I was still attached to my lead. I say my lead because I really should mention that Belle is perhaps not the best-trained dog, and she doesn't quite get the idea that the lead is supposed to control her movements. Instead, she thinks it is some kind of human tow-rope that she can use to drag me around the English countryside, and the muddier that countryside is, the better.

I realized what Belle had seen when I spied half a dozen rabbits dotted along the hillside to our right, which is actually called Lady Hill. They scattered as soon as I saw them, presumably in anticipation of a big fluffy dog dragging some poor schmuck up the hill, but at the last minute, I managed to regain control of the situation and found to my delight that I was only moderately covered in mud, and only up to my knees or so.

Lady Hill has a long and interesting history, at least for what seems to be, at the end of the day, a pretty small hill. It is actually a relic of the ice age, an almost perfectly formed half egg shape of a hill commonly called a drumlin, apparently, and was formed by a moving glacier many moons ago.

The hill is topped with several Scots Pines, planted for the diamond jubilee of Queen Victoria in 1897, which celebrated 60 years on the throne for the elderly monarch. The jubilee was a big deal at the time, with the queen being the first-ever British monarch to last that long. Dignitaries arrived at Buckingham Palace from all around the world, Union Flags draped buildings in the north, south, east and west, street parties and bonfires lit up the land and pubs were given special dispensation to stay open until 2.30 am. Oh, and up here, they planted some trees.

I'm not sure whose idea it had been to plant some trees, but perhaps we should be grateful, as of course nowadays we need more trees than ever, so please accept my apologies for being a grumpy old grouch when it comes to planting trees for the queen.

Anyway, the hill has yet more fascinating history. If you look, you will see a tumbling wall built completely around it. This wall served a purpose, or at least it used to, and it was basically a rabbit prison. Actually, it was two rabbit prisons, with the idea of keeping a few very select black-furred rabbits on the inside while simultaneously keeping every other rabbit in the world most firmly on the outside.

This was the creation of a man called Frank Sayer-Graham, who lived at Heather Cottage back in Aysgarth, which we had passed earlier while on the bus. He kept a special breed of rabbit here, which started out as black but then turned silver as they grew older. Silver fur was heavily prized, and Frank managed to make a small fortune selling these pelts to the rich and famous, and he is even said to have supplied furs to the last Tsar of Russia, Nicholas II.

In his day, Frank would have exported the pelts from the animals all around the world, with them starting their journey on the Wensleydale Railway, which we were currently following, of course, and which runs just a few feet south of Lady Hill.

The wall, as I already mentioned, is now crumbling, which is probably why the rabbits that we had just seen are no longer black and silver but brown and white, indicating that the wild rabbits eventually broke into Lady Hill and did exactly what rabbits do best, which is to make more rabbits, of course.

Frank must have done pretty well in his business because Heather Cottage had been a very nice house indeed, though I find it hard to imagine making a fortune from rabbits.

As Lady Hill slowly receded into the distance behind us, the railway line seemed to come and go to our north. Parts of it were flanked with a line of old-growth trees atop a high ridge, while other sections of it seemed to have simply ceased to exist and had vanished back into the landscape.

Belle, still off her lead in this apparently sheep-free zone, seemed to be covering at least three miles for each one I managed, darting this way and that and sniffing everything she came across, and once or twice she ventured down to the riverbank on our left. The river was still big and wide here and looked equally deep though it was really hard to tell, so every time she went near it, I had to call her back, and for once, she actually listened to me. Perhaps she realized that this river was a bit too much, even for an expert swimmer such as her.

Around half a mile after Lady Hill, we came to another small river, probably about fifteen feet wide or so, which emptied into the larger River Ure to our left. It was too big to jump across and looked quite deep, and just as I was wondering how we would get cross, and as we arrived immediately next to it, I saw that someone had conveniently built some stepping stones to allow passage.

These stepping stones were huge, and whoever put them here

seems to have used half a dozen large oil drums or barrels and filled them with concrete. They made a very effective crossing, and I was soon over them without incident, and while Belle looked a bit hesitant, I was certain she would follow me across. However, when I got to the other side and looked back, she was still stood there, on the other riverbank, looking warily at the stepping stones.

I shouted for her to come to me a couple of times and was considering going back to get her when she finally took a first tentative step. Unfortunately, she stepped into the water, and I had to shout to her to stop and use the stepping stones right in front of her.

Eventually, she put one of her paws on the first stone and began to cross. As I said, the stones were huge and made for a good and easy crossing, but nonetheless, Belle did not seem so sure. She passed over the first stone and onto the second, and all the while, I continued shouting words of encouragement, but then for some inexplicable reason, she jumped off, straight into the deep water below.

At least she would finally get that wash, I thought, as I watched her happily swim around in circles in the deep pool, biting and snapping at the water as she went. She ignored my calls to come on out for quite some time, and it was only when I started to walk away from her that she finally and reluctantly emerged from the water, which was exactly when I realized I was in the danger zone.

Dogs, you see, any dog, in fact, do one thing when they come out of water. They shake. Belle normally does this after having a bath, so I have cunningly evolved a method where I wrap her in a very large blanket as soon as she is out of the water, carry her through the house, and deposit her in the garden. Then, I re-move the towel and simply run. If I am lucky and manage to put some distance between myself and the hound, I only get a mild drenching. I can then usually manage to dry myself off after a short summer and a combination of a bundle of towels and a couple of hairdryers. Occasionally though, when I am simply not fast enough, or when Belle thinks I am playing some sort of game by running off and she decides to chase me, I instead get a thorough soaking, but it's nothing that the local water company can't sort out with a few sandbags and a flood warning.

Today, luckily, it was only a mild drenching, and my jacket took the brunt of it, though I imagined that I would smell like a wet dog for at least the rest of the day.

We continued our course westwards, with Belle occasionally going on her lead due to sheep, and in one field in particular, a rather large flock of them took a distinct liking to Belle. I'm not sure what it was, but they followed us for a good few hundred yards, and it was rather comical.

I had noticed that Belle was walking exactly next to me and would not leave my side, as she can normally be a bit of a puller when on her lead. I stopped and looked around, at which time around two dozen Swaledale sheep, huddled together very closely indeed, also ground to a complete halt, and I'm sure they looked away from me so I would not notice them. We moved off again, Belle apparently glued to my knees, and out of the corner of my eye behind me, I saw the flock begin to move after us, almost as a single entity rather than two dozen separate cotton wool balls.

This continued for a few minutes, with the sheep stopping as we stopped and following us again every time we started moving. I must admit that I turned this into a bit of a game, but anyway, it is the most fun I have had with sheep since my brother in law's stag night in Wales.

Although I was having lots of fun, Belle was very unnerved by all of this, and I really thought her a bit of a coward. However, in retrospect, she is a city dog, and it was true that she was heavily outnumbered, even if they were only sheep. I wondered what she would make of a cow when she saw one?

Moving on, Nappa Hall lay somewhere to the north, just over the brow of the hill, and is described by English Heritage as possibly the finest unspoilt fortified manor house in the north of England. I had hoped we would be able to see it from the path, but if you could, I missed it. Mary Queen of Scots was briefly imprisoned in the house before being moved to Bolton Castle, but more of that later.

I have seen it before, though, and from a distance, the house looks more like a castle, and I found myself envying whoever lived there today. I can just imagine the lord of the manor popping out every morning and shooting a couple of peasants, who are of course otherwise known as ramblers, before continuing on with his merry day of counting money and shoving it under his mattress before chasing the maid around the kitchen for a while. I'm sure those days are long gone, of course, but you never know.

There is, however, supposed to be a bit of a ghost problem at the hall. A figure has often been seen wearing a black velvet dress, and it is said that this is actually Mary Queen of Scots herself.

Like much of Wensleydale, the Nappa Estate had originally been owned by the Scrope family, but at some point in the 1300s, Richard le Scrope, the 1st Baron Scrope of Bolton, gave it away to a presumably good mate of his, a man called James Metcalf.

However, it was James' son Thomas who finally built the hall, and he did a very good job of it too. He had to, of course, as back in those days, those pesky border reivers would continually pop down from Scotland for the mediaeval equivalent of a booze cruise, stealing anything and everything that they could get their hands on before dragging it straight back up to bonny Scotland with them.

The house stayed within the Metcalf family for some centuries, though at one time there was at least a hint of sour grapes when the Scrope family tried to regain the house through the courts, but after a nice bit of bribery, the judge let the house stay with the Metcalfs after all.

And what is the point of having a hall and an estate without having a coat of arms? The answer is none, which is why the Metcalf family soon got theirs, and it featured three rather well-pizzled calves. Don't know what pizzled means? Don't worry, I didn't either, but it basically means penis. A rather surprising number of coats of arms feature prominent penises, which is something I had never really noticed before. To be honest, it should be said that I had never actually looked that close, but then why would you? Apparently, Henry VII made this tradition quite a trendy one after the Battle of Bosworth Field in 1485. The British Royal Family carries it on to this day. Who knew?

Anyway, things finally went pear-shaped for the Metcalfs, and they were ultimately forced to sell the house in the 1700s. It then passed through one or two other families who did their best to keep it in good condition, and some work was even done to restore it, so when the house came once again under the ownership of the Metcalfs, who moved back in as tenants in 1889 and finally bought it back in 1930, it was in as good a condition as it had ever been.

Sadly, the Metcalfs once again sold the house in 2008, but whoever owns it today is still clearly doing an excellent job of looking after it, so I expect it will be there for some years to come.

We left the meadow and found ourselves climbing up the steep embankment of the railway line. The path never went this way, but I just wanted to have a look. I had wondered if it was possible to walk on top of the old track bed, but when I got to the top of the bank, I found it completely overgrown. Although the trees were small and scattered, meaning it would technically be possible to make your way along the top, it would certainly not be a comfortable walk.

We scrambled back down into the field, with Belle covering

the distance in half the time it took me, and after climbing over a style that was certainly not built for dogs, meaning I had to carry my flabby friend over it, we found ourselves almost at Nappa Mill.

It was here where two things dawned on me. The first was that I had not seen a single sign that pointed the way on this walk, and the second was that we had not seen any people yet. I mentioned this to Belle, but she just stared at me with all of the interest of a dead badger, so we carried on.

How surprised was I, then, when we met an older couple out walking at the mill. They were on holiday up here and originally hailed from Northampton and said they were having a wild time up here in the dales. Fans of *All Creatures Great and Small*, they were spending a leisurely week exploring the area and visiting some of the places used for filming. This is probably why they had decided to use Grassington as their base, which is where much of the new series is filmed.

I told them about our walk, which they knew of but had not done, and I told them about my lazy mates who had come up with all sorts of excuses not to come. I also mentioned that I intended to write a book about this walk and told them about the other walks I had written about. I must admit it was just a blatant attempt at a bit of shameless and free publicity, so how surprised was I when they said their son was a writer, and he was called Jules Howard. I was a little bit stunned, as I have one of his books, although technically it belongs to my son. He writes about animals and nature, and they make great Christmas presents. Isn't it amazing who you meet when you are out and about, I thought, as I walked away after our little chat, which had been cut short by a sudden shower.

Unfortunately, we moved on in the wrong direction, which I blamed Belle for, as I had been reading the map so far, and I decided it was now her turn. After a hundred yards or so, however, I realized my mistake, and we turned around, which is when we bumped into the old couple again who had also decided to turn around. They told me that they had been to the mill and it was a dead-end, but after checking my map, which clearly showed a path, I decided to go there anyway. I shouted to them that I would see them in the King's Arms at Askrigg and that it was their round, but they pretended not to hear me.

The path was hidden on the right-hand side of a large barn and was barely visible, so it is easy to understand how they had missed it. Soon through it, we found ourselves in a large empty field, so Belle was once again off her lead and running in all directions one after the other and again heading directly for the river.

This was the River Ure again and looked just as wide and deep as it had a mile back, so I called to her not to go into the water, and she surprisingly obeyed once again. Instead, she happily sniffed along the riverbank and thankfully did not roll in anything brown, and she still seemed to be remarkably clean following her bath in the river a while back.

The path was dead straight and easy to follow here, and we were soon across it after which, and for only the second time today, we found ourselves back on a road, this time heading towards Worton, which is actually a slight deviation from the Herriot way but worthwhile nonetheless.

As we got to Worton Bridge, which crosses the River Ure to the south, I asked Belle if she fancied a quick trip to the Victoria Arms. She never said no, so off we trundled over the modern-looking structure in search of the pub in this tiny village.

However, just after we crossed the bridge, Belle almost yanked me off my feet as she suddenly ground to a halt without informing me first. She can be like that sometimes. I turned around to see what was so interesting and saw that she was transfixed at something in the road.

At first, I couldn't see anything, but on a second look, there was a tiny baby bird under a tree and in the middle of the road.

This perhaps explained the rather noisy one that was in the tree above and was currently going just a little bit mental.

At the same time, I heard a car approaching and thinking on my feet, I went over to the little thing to have a look. It did have feathers but was clearly very young, and it just looked up at me with its big dopey eyes.

Belle sniffed the air around it but dared not come too close, presumably as she had no idea what it was or whether it had claws and liked the taste of city dogs. As the car got closer, I made the quick decision to move it off the road and scooped it up in my hands.

It did not struggle but just sat there, and as I placed it on the grass verge, with Belle looking on obediently with clear curiosity in her eyes, the car that had been approaching sped rapidly past, right over the spot where the little creature had just been sat.

Mother continued to go absolutely crazy and was now flying around, so Belle and I backed off. We then saw her fly straight down to her little chick, and she appeared to be telling it off. She was probably saying something along the lines of *you're grounded*, but anyway, we left them to it and moved away.

It's actually a myth that most birds will abandon their young if you touch them, by the way, as they don't have a great sense of smell. Think about it. When was the last time you saw a bird with a nose? Anyway, regardless of this, I figured that the little chick definitely had a better chance in life so long as it managed to avoid being rolled out like pastry on the tarmac of this road, though we will never know of course whether this particular one managed to make it back up to its nest or not.

The centre of the village wasn't difficult to find. After a short walk through a couple of fields where yet more Swaledale sheep eyed Belle with more than a hint of suspicion, a shallow uphill struggle took us straight into the heart of the village.

Unfortunately, the pub wasn't in the heart of the village but was on the main road beyond it to the south, but as we had come this far, we plodded on, taking one for the team. Belle's four legs carried her better than my two, and after a few more minutes, we finally arrived at the pub, ducking under the low door into the Aladdin's Cave that was promised on the other side.

I had read many good things about this pub, with the main one being that it had been run by one man since way back in 1956. Now I don't know about you, but if I had been involved in something since 1956, then I would imagine that I probably loved whatever it was, which tells me that this pub had been well looked after.

That man was called Ralph Daykin, and he had indeed spent more than half a century looking after the Victoria Arms along with his wife, Pat. It was not only their business, but I had read that the bar also doubled as their living room when the place was closed.

The pub was famous locally not only for the hospitality that lay within but also for the generosity of both staff and patrons, and it was within these walls that tens of thousands of pounds had been raised over the years for various good causes. Furthermore, had you come in here on a cold wintry night, then you might well have had no chance whatsoever of getting near to the roaring fire that was always lit, as you would, in fact, have found orphaned lambs curled up in wicker baskets and being cared for by the staff in order to get them through the cold dark nights. I did wonder to myself momentarily how many of those lambs later ended up on the menu, but that's life, I guess.

All in all, it is reckoned that Ralph Daykin was one of Britain's longest-serving licensees, serving countless pints here for a staggering 56 years until he sadly passed away in 2013.

What we found inside was even better than expected. This pub must have been ancient, with low timbered ceilings instantly transporting us back a couple of centuries. All sorts of ornaments and decorations had been stuck around the pub over the decades, with money and postcards from all around the world interspersed with mounted fox and stag's heads, as well as old lamps, plates and medals.

I went to the bar and ordered a pint of coke while Belle found a comfy spot on a rug directly in front of a roaring open fire, and it did not seem to bother her that there was already someone sitting there. Sitting down on a pew that presumably had once been in a nearby church, it was a pleasure to rest my feet and warm up, and I imagined that Belle would be thinking exactly the same thing, if she were able to think such things, that is.

We only stayed for around ten or fifteen minutes and had soon headed back through the village and down the hill back to Worton Bridge, where we re-joined the Herriot Way, although again, there were no signs to point the way. It had not been a long walk to the pub, while a drink and the chance to warm up a little had definitely been worth it, and the whole venture had added less than a mile to our journey.

Back on the path, someone had kindly laid rather a lot of flagstones end to end, which made for a great path through what was otherwise quite a marshy looking field. They had managed to do so in a dead straight line as well, which was pretty impressive, so we soon managed to get to the far corner, where Belle had to once again go back on her lead because of an infestation of several dozen sheep.

These were more Swaledales, and like the others we had encountered earlier, they did not seem to be afraid of Belle and were, in fact, very inquisitive. They followed us as a large group, bleating noisily behind us, and came even closer than the other gang of their fellow mates had earlier. They got so close that Belle growled quietly to herself, clearly on edge. They were only a couple of feet away from us, and I could see their eyes, which were weird.

Rather than having round pupils, sheep have elongated pupils that look like long slits. I already knew this, but what I did not know and had never seen, or at least noticed, is that as one of the sheep near us lowered its head to take a bite of some fresh and tasty grass, the slits remained level with the ground, and this is what looked a bit weird.

Even more strangely, there was one sheep who stood out from all the rest. If I were to name him, I would probably call him Mike Tyson. He was built of nothing but muscles, looked very mean, and was wearing either a body camera or some sort of tracking device. He came the closest of the lot, and at one point, I thought he was going to charge, but he must have decided we were not a threat. He did, however, follow us for quite a while, and it seemed as if he was making sure we definitely left his patch. As we walked away, I thought to myself that this was the first time I had ever felt threatened by a bloody sheep. I'll get my own back, I thought. I'll have lamb for dinner on Sunday.

As we stood and stared at these sheep, it started raining, and although it was not too heavy, I put my hat on nonetheless. Belle also had a coat, which was currently languishing at the bottom of my rucksack, but I had not put it on her as she was not too keen on wearing it. If the rain continued, however, I vowed to wrestle her to the ground and make her wear it, and to hell with her sharp teeth, I thought to myself.

We again found ourselves scrambling up the embankment that had once carried the railway, though we did not join it but merely crossed it at an angle. Askrigg was clearly in sight at the top of this hill, and while it wasn't necessarily a big hill, I was definitely out of breath by the time we got to the top.

With Belle back on her lead, we passed through a small gate onto Silver Street, a narrow lane lined with old stone houses that were very pleasing to the eye and which took us directly to the main street in Askrigg, which funnily enough, was called Main Street.

Askrigg is a very pretty little village, with a couple of pubs and a cobbled marketplace surrounded by pleasant townhouses, and if you are really lucky you might just visit on one of the many days when sheep are driven through the streets, which is an absolutely awesome sight, trust me.

If Askrigg looks familiar, it is possibly because it was one of the original locations used in the first television series of *All Creatures Great and Small,* where it temporarily became Darrowby. In particular, the house almost opposite where the church is and on the corner of Silver Street, which we had just passed, was used as a stand-in for the vet's surgery of Skeldale House but was originally known as Cringley House. Not surprisingly, new owners have now officially changed its name to Skeldale House in order to capitalize on the television show as much as possible, and I do not blame them one bit.

Just opposite Skeldale House and the cross, another house that is set back from the street marks the site of the former Old Hall. It was a magnificent four-storey building dating back to 1678, with balconies on the upper floors, but it was unfortunately burnt down by a pyromaniac in 1935, which is a real shame.

One of the village pubs, the King's Arms, also became famous when it doubled as the Drover's Arms in the television series, which, let's face it, must really annoy the owners of the other pub in the village, The Crown. However, unlike Cringley House, the King's Arms has not changed its name, but then it doesn't need to, as it does very well on passing tourists who come here to see it anyway.

In the spirit of supporting local businesses, of course, we head straight for this pub, and thankfully this means a walk of just fifty yards. This pub is just as nice as the last one back in Worton, though it is certainly somewhat less cluttered. From the ceiling hang not money and postcards, but hooks, possibly for the hanging of exhausted or maybe even dead ramblers, I ponder, but the barman tells me they were, in fact, used for hanging horse riding tackle back in the day.

Belle immediately found her spot on the flagstone floor directly in front of the large roaring fire. I apologized to the man who was already sitting there, though he welcomed her in regardless and then beckoned me to sit down too. I think he thought I was apologizing because Belle had just barged in between him and the fire, but I was actually apologizing because she smelt like the business end of a skunk, which only became more pronounced as she gently sizzled away in front of the flames. She lay sprawled across the floor for a while before soon moving slightly further away from the heat when it became too much and curled up into a tight ball.

Apparently, dogs curl up to preserve warmth and to protect their vital organs from things that are hungry and have sharp teeth, a leftover relic from wilder days, it is said.

As I sat down, I looked around for the couple we had seen near Nappa Mill, but they were nowhere in sight, which was a shame because it was their round.

The man we had joined, who was now incidentally stroking my smelly dog, is local, he tells me, and is waiting for his friends, and after I get my drink from the bar, he goes on to tell me some of the filthiest jokes I have ever heard, though none of which I will repeat here. He then goes on to tell me that he also knows lots of jokes about unemployed people, but none of them work, which is one I will remember, I decide, and will use on everyone I meet and which will probably annoy my kids very much.

There are some nice pictures on the walls, many of which feature the cast of the first series of *All Creatures Great and Small*, and I am particularly drawn to one featuring Peter Davison as Tristan Farnon, Siegfried's socially adventurous and somewhat untamed younger brother, but more of him later.

There are also some rather interesting historical photos of the pub. I noticed them as I popped to the toilet, and as usual, I managed to get lost and inadvertently explored more or less the whole building before I managed to find the gents. When I came back into the bar area, Belle was enjoying yet another belly rub from a complete stranger and barely noticed my return and hadn't missed me all that much either, by all accounts.

Unfortunately, we could not stay in here all day, and after calling Belle around a million times, she finally gave up her warm spot in front of the fire and sauntered back over to me. With her lead back on, we left the pub, and I think we were both happy to discover that it had stopped raining.

We wandered back towards the church and stopped at the stone cross on the cobblestone floor. If you look carefully at the cobbles, there is a large iron ring set into them, and this is called the bullring. In days gone by, bull baiting was a common occurrence, with a bull being tied up here and set upon by dogs with men betting on the outcome. It was later used for another kind of fight. If a villager, or anyone else for that matter, fancied a bit of a punch up, they could turn the bull ring over and then wait for someone else to turn it back over again, which signified that both parties were then ready for a good old-fashioned scrap. To be honest, I imagined that this sort of thing still goes on every Saturday night in most parts of England.

I tied Belle to the ring while I took a couple of photos, but was very careful not to turn it over, lest some local jump out from behind the wall and beat the living daylights out of me. Photo in hand, I grabbed Belle, and we wandered off towards Mill Lane. When no one was looking, and as we were leaving, I turned the bull ring over and ran.

We passed some newer houses as we left the village, and I imagined it would be a very nice place to live and briefly considered moving here, though I also imagined it would probably be rather expensive to do so. When I later checked, I had been right; there was nothing around here for less than a third of a million pounds, which is absolutely crazy when you think about it. This caused me to quickly shelve any and all plans of upping sticks and coming to live in the dales, at least until that lottery win came in.

One of the occupants of these newer houses had gone to great pains to decorate their garden. They had presumably done this for Halloween, as the decorations included such delights as a human skull stuck on a pole and a life-sized skeleton sitting on a garden bench unless, of course, it was actually the remains of a hiker who had simply given up at some point in the distant past.

They had also built a mini art gallery and a library for passers-by to use, and while I had a quick look at the artwork on display, which was actually pretty good but could perhaps be described as minimalist, I did not bother with the library.

I don't think Belle was a fan of the artwork, though, as I saw her going to the toilet on it, so I thought it best to move on. I have noticed that she can be a bit of a philistine like that.

At the end of the village, we encountered what is possibly the narrowest gate in Yorkshire. It certainly wasn't built for us tubbies, and as I looked at it, I doubted that I would ever get through it without some form of major surgery, either on me or on the gate.

Belle just managed to squeeze through when I opened it, but it was a bit more complicated for me. With a combination of lifting my rucksack up, for it was my rucksack that was the problem and not my big fat belly, honest, I somehow managed to squeeze through at an angle, popping out on the other side in a sudden, explosive burst that propelled me some way across the field. I was actually somewhat surprised at having made it at all, to be honest. If I had become stuck, it could have been days before anyone came along and discovered me, I pondered. Belle wouldn't have helped, she would have just sat there, and in fact, she might even have eaten me after a few days. Apparently, dogs do that; they will actually eat you when you die if they are locked in the house with you at the time. Cats are worse, though. They will literally eat your face off in no time at all, even before you are technically dead, so be warned.

Once again, a straight flagstone path led the way, at least for a while, until we disappeared through another impossibly narrow gate and into some woods. A sign pointed to Mill Gill Force, one of today's highlights by all accounts, being a high waterfall consisting of an impressive high cascade as well as some lower falls.

Mill Gill force, then, became our next destination, and it is one of the best-kept secrets in Yorkshire, or so the tourist guides tantalizingly promise us, I tell Belle. However, while I think she's looking forward to splashing in the water and will probably not appreciate the waterfall, I will certainly appreciate it for her.

The path twisted and turned through the trees, and while I carefully navigated my way along, trying not to break an ankle on the tree roots that poked this way and that and which repeatedly tried to snag my feet, Belle was once again in her element, dashing through the forest as fast as anything I had seen.

You do technically have to leave the Herriot Way to view the waterfalls, but it is such a small diversion, it is almost ridiculous. It took less than a minute to get there from the main path, making this the second worthwhile addition of the day.

Belle, of course, was straight into the water at the falls, splashing about and biting at it as she does. I did not stop her for two reasons. Firstly, the water here did not look dangerous, so there was little risk of her being carried away, and secondly, she was still pretty stinky and needed more of a wash.

Three people are admiring the waterfall when we get there, a man and two women. I ask the ladies if they are twins, but they blush and tell me they are mother and daughter. Perhaps they presumed I was being all jokey and probably thought I knew they were mother and daughter, but I honestly thought they were twins, being so alike as they were. Clearly a lot older than me, this probably explains my inability to tell their ages apart. I'm not sure about you, but old people just look, well, old, and it can be really hard to guess someone's age. I imagine that my kids say the same about people my age.

They are from Wakefield and have brought their accents to prove it, and they tell me that they can tell I am from Hull because of my accent, which is odd because I don't have an accent, I tell them. We all have a little laugh at this, and then I remember the joke about the unemployed people, which did not go down too well with them, to be honest, which more or less signals the end of the conversation.

The waterfall tumbles merrily down what is a very rocky and incredibly pretty ravine, and while it bears no claim to being the tallest waterfall or any other record, it is still very nice to look at. Belle does indeed appreciate the water, and for a minute, she splashed about as if trying to catch a nice brown trout, but once again, it appears she is just a bit stupid and is, in fact, merely biting the water. I guess she was dropped at birth or something. Popping her back on her lead, it is time to move on, but not before she generously shares with me all of the water she has collected in the form of a free shower, just as I had more or less dried out from the earlier rain. With me now also dripping wet from head to foot, we plod on.

A sign pointed to yet another waterfall another half a mile or so further along the path, but given the distance we still had to cover, I decided against it, as there were other things that I would rather see instead, but I vowed to return another day to have a look.

Because of my little detour, I now found myself heading south back to the actual route of the Herriot Way. There were still no signs pointing the way, and when I left the woods and entered a farmer's field, I came across a sign that was actually broken, with the fingerpost snapped off and missing. However, I could see which direction it had previously pointed, so I decided to go that way anyway.

A farmer had been rounding sheep up with a quad bike and a sheepdog, which I thought was a fantastic fusion of old and new technologies, and I had been watching them curiously as I walked, always fascinated by how they do this. The dogs seem to know what the farmer wants, even without the whistles and the shouts, and I always think they look like they are enjoying themselves when they are working, and I don't just mean the dogs.

When he had finished, the farmer bounced across the field in my direction, and I instinctively presumed I was either trespassing or he wanted me to open the gate. I opened it anyway, as it was also the direction I was going. I gestured for him to go first, but instead, he stopped and killed the engine.

It turns out that he had seen me looking at the map and had wondered if I was lost and needed any help. I advised him that I wasn't and I didn't, as I was walking the Herriot Way, which made him laugh, as it turns out, in fact, that I was lost and I did indeed need some help. The gate I had opened and intended to go through would lead me in the opposite direction, he said, and I actually wanted to be through another gate, which he kindly pointed out for me.

As we chatted, I decided to ask him about the sheep's eyes, namely what the hell was going on with them, and I am glad to say that he knew the answer. Sheep, he told me, are basically prey, which first of all is why they have their eyes on the side of their head, something that gives them the largest field of view possible.

Their elongated slits are just that and give them the best view of the ground, as there is not much need for them to see any higher, which makes sense when you think about it. The most amazing thing, though, is that their eyeballs automatically rotate as they lower and raise their heads, with the slits keeping more or less parallel with the ground, something which I found truly amazing.

To fully comprehend the wonderful trickery that is going on here, it would be the equivalent of you looking directly at the ground below you and still being able to see the rather large and scary wolf that is currently sneaking up behind you with lunch on its mind. There is a name for this, too, he said, and that is cyclovergence, and it is something that horses and deer are also pretty good at. It's amazing what you learn when you just stop and talk for a while, I thought.

All through our conversation, his incredibly well-behaved black and white sheepdog had been sat obediently on the back of his quad bike, while Belle had cowered behind me with her tail tucked in.

I thanked him before he sped off, and when Belle slowly emerged from behind me, and after I called her a coward, we carried on with our walk, now confident of going in the actual right direction. I'm not sure where we would have ended up had he not been there, but luckily, he was, and that is all that counts. It's strange, though, that at the point where you get lost, and you don't even know it, someone turns up and points you in the right direction. In a rare moment of deep philosophy, this could apply to life when you think about it.

We head downhill to Helm, which is basically just a farm-house, and pass some spaceships that seem to have landed in the next field. Strange looking metal things with four legs, there are three spaced quite close together, leaving me somewhat puzzled as to what they are.

The small village of Bainbridge lay just less than a mile or so to the south, so I suggested to Belle once again that we should go and find out if there is a pub there, purely in the spirit of supporting local businesses again, you understand. Once again, Belle never objected, which I actually took as a ringing endorse-ment of my cunning plan, so for the second time today, we headed south in search of refreshments and a quick rest.

Yet another doctor would have once walked these roads, a man called John Fothergill, who, if you remember rightly, was the subject of a book by Sir Christopher Booth. Fothergill was born in Bainbridge in the 1700s and went on to become the father of mouth-to-mouth ventilation, giving the first known lecture on it in 1745. If you remember, he was also best mates with Benjamin Franklin, but I'm not sure how that worked, so maybe it was a long-distance thing.

While we are on the subject of doctors, we might as well get the rest of them out of the way because the 18th and 19th centuries saw this tiny little part of the country give us an absurd number of them who all went on to change the world with their medical knowledge.

Robert Willan is the next one, who was born here in 1757 and who more or less invented the field of dermatology, that is, skin conditions, describing impetigo, lupus and psoriasis, and in fact, he was the first person ever known to have used the word lupus, so he maybe thought it up himself one day, who knows. He was also a pioneer in the world of eating disorders, which surprises me, as I never knew that eating disorders existed in the 1700s, chiefly because there was never any bloody food. Willan was the recipient of the Fothergill Gold Medal, whatever that was, although it was certainly nothing to do with John Fothergill. It is probably worth pointing out that Willan was in esteemed company with this award, though, with one of the later winners of the medal being none other than Edward Jenner for his pioneering work on vaccines, for which we are all doubly grateful for nowadays, I expect. Anyway, this hopefully helps to demonstrate that the medal was a pretty big deal, even back then.

Anthony Fothergill is the next one, and while he was a friend of John Fothergill, he was not, perhaps surprisingly, any obvious relation, though again he was born around these parts in 1732. He soon became quite an authority on reviving the victims of drowning, establishing many practices that are still in use today. Fothergill also made rather a lot of money, and I mean a lot, so was able to retire to Philadelphia in the good old United States, but had to flee back to England in 1812, basically so he would not die, I imagine. This was because of *The War of 1812*, when Fothergill suddenly found himself in a country he was technically at war with, and one which was particularly upset with English people, possibly because we had just burned down their nice new White House.

Unfortunately, however, more or less as soon as he returned to England, he died anyway, which is not surprising considering this was the 1800s and he was over 80-years-old, at a time when the average life span was only around 40 years or so. In his rather large will that he left behind, he bequeathed a vast sum of money to the London Medical Society in order to set up the Fothergillian Prize, which is awarded to whoever knocks up the best essay on any given topic, and which answers the question posed by Robert Willan a few moments ago.

William Hillary is the next one, and I am sorry about this, I had no idea there could possibly be so many pioneering doctors from this neck of the woods. I won't go into details on him because we'll come across him later, but his story is still interesting nonetheless, so you'll have to wait and see.

John Haygarth was another one, born in Garsdale, and is yet another amazing doctor who went on to change the world. His speciality was finding new ways to prevent diseases from spreading, which was particularly concerning during his life in the 1700s due to the prevalence of smallpox. He was, for instance, one of the strongest advocates of inoculation, which was actually quite unpopular at the time. This unpopularity is perhaps better understood when you consider that the best form of inoculation at the time was variolation, which basically means taking body fluids from an infected person and sticking it into another with a rather pointy thing in the hope of triggering an immune response. I assume that if I chased you down the street with a syringe full of cowpox, you would run like hell; well, that was what was basically going on at the time.

One positive and more welcome idea that Haygarth came up with, and one that seems common sense nowadays, was separating patients with any given illness or fever from healthy people, and you have to wonder why it took millions of years of evolution to figure this out, but there you go.

What Haygarth really earned his pocket money from, though, was the world's first demonstration of the placebo effect, which showed how people could be healed by something that, when closely examined, had no medicinal value whatsoever.

This started with something called the Perkins' Tractor, invented by American Elisha Perkins in the late 1700s, although invented is perhaps being a bit generous. Imagine a metal stick 3-inches long, somewhat resembling a magic wand or a drum stick, though with the far end sharp and pointy. Perkins claimed they were made from a secret alloy, though they were actually made of simple steel and brass. He also claimed that by passing it over an ailing body part, his tractor could literally suck out the illness from the body, hence the name, which came from the old meaning of the word tractor, which means *to pull.*

Though many in the medical community immediately saw Perkins and his so-called tractor for what they were, which was quackery, his aggressive marketing campaign nonetheless saw thousands sold, particularly after he advertised them in The Times at the price of 5 guineas a set. Even George Washington, the first president of the United States, bought one of these strange but ultimately useless contraptions.

Haygarth, then, arrived at the party somewhat late, in 1799. What he did was to make his own tractors, although he cunningly and sneakily made his of wood but failed to inform his patients, who in fact thought they were being treated with genuine tractors, made of those rare and fantastical alloys, remember. He used them on five people, and four reported improvements, and when he repeated the experiment the next day, the results were exactly the same.

This was the first clear demonstration of the placebo effect, and it was further illustrated when Haygarth used both sets of tractors to treat sick animals. I shouldn't need to say this, as I hope you have figured it out already, but there were no visible improvements in any of the animals, purely and simply because they had absolutely no idea what was going on and had no preconceived notions regarding their treatment. Haygarth went on to suggest that this is also why famous doctors are often more successful than ones that are unknown, and he even proposed that much of the medicine of the day did, in fact, rely greatly on the placebo effect.

What is perhaps most interesting about this little story, though, is how it ends. Towards the end of 1799, and amidst an outbreak of yellow fever in New York, Perkins claimed to have found a cure for this dreadful disease, though his supposed cure turned out to be nothing more than vinegar with a bit of extra acid thrown in. Not surprisingly, while treating his patients, Perkins caught the disease more or less straight away, which soon advanced to the toxic phase, and he was dead within a fortnight.

That's about enough of old dead doctors, and it really was time to move on, and anyway, Belle was looking a little bit bored.

The road took us over the River Ure at Yore Bridge and then ran parallel with the River Bain, incidentally one of the shortest named rivers in the whole country, at less than five miles long.

Furthermore, Fors Abbey once stood just on the riverbank to the east of Yore Bridge, but there is no sign of it now. It was the monks of Jervaulx Abbey that actually started out here, but they can't have been very happy with this site because as soon as Jervaulx became available, they were off like a shot. This may be because Fors was said to be haunted, and the monks here would often have their torches blown out inexplicably, although when you think about it, it was probably just a bit draughty. Either way, they soon moved on.

The monks immediately recognized the fertile land around the dale and the holy order soon amassed thousands of acres of it, planting on the lowlands and grazing sheep in the mountains. Being built of wood, the original abbey was soon gone and mostly forgotten, or at least it was until the railway line arrived.

While they slowly built it, the navvies managed to dig up lots of lovely skeletons at the site where the old abbey once stood, and these skeletons were presumed to be the ancient monks of Fors Abbey itself.

The River Bain, then, actually emerges from Semerwater, a lake of quite some fame, less than five miles away, and flows into the larger River Ure just west of the bridge we have most recently crossed and quite near to the site of the abbey.

Semerwater is actually famous for allegedly being the site of a lost city. Legend has it that, many moons ago, an angel in disguise arrived there searching for food and drink on a dark and stormy night. Going from door to door of many prosperous houses and being turned away from every single one, he eventually arrived at a hovel housing an old couple on a hill overlooking the so-called city. They took him in despite being poor, fed him and gave him drinks, and later, when it was time to leave, the angel turned to the city and cursed it, causing waters to rise up immediately, engulfing all of the rich houses and leaving only the old couple in their hovel as thanks for their kindness. This story was famously turned into the *Ballad of Semerwater* by Sir William Watson.

Moving on, we soon sniffed out the Rose and Crown in the centre of the village. After Belle had had her fill of some doggy water which had kindly been placed at the door and which would ensure we would not need to curse the pub to a watery end, we walked in and found a very snug little bar indeed.

I had recently checked some online reviews for this pub, some of which were terrible. One even went so far as to describe the manager as Basil Fawlty, so I instantly knew that I would absolutely love this place. It was very nice, and the staff were incredibly helpful, and Belle once again laid herself out in front of the fire and warmed her belly. Completely pushing in front of everyone else who was also trying to warm their cockles, as was now her habit, it seems, she enjoyed belly rub after belly rub and became very popular indeed, although I did note that no one offered to buy her a drink. Anyway, my point is, don't necessarily take any notice of the reviews, as unfortunately there was no sign of Basil Fawlty, which was a real shame.

By the way, the pub's name celebrates the end of the Wars of the Roses when Henry Tudor united the red rose of Lancaster with the white rose of York by marrying Elizabeth of York. By then, pubs had a legal obligation to hang a sign outside, which directly resulted in many pub names which we are still so familiar with today, some of us more than others, of course. I pride myself in this regard, but only in the interest of supporting local businesses, you understand.

This tradition of pub naming had actually started way back in 1393 when the king, Richard II, ordered signage to make them more easily identifiable. To be absolutely truthful, this was because most of the population were illiterate, so an illustration had to be used instead.

In the case of King Richard, his royal symbol was a white hart. Thus, pubs called The White Hart became and remain very popular. A white hart, in case you did not know, is an incredibly rare white red deer stag, and its colour, or actually lack of colour, is the result of a medical condition that causes its hair and skin to lose their original hue. There, you learn something new every day. Anyway, as I have already said, pubs called the White Hart are still very common today, coming fourth after the Red Lion, the Crown and the Royal Oak, and Belle and I intend to try them all.

Incidentally, while we are on the subject of Richard II, it is probably fair to say that he was a bit of a nutter, and perhaps the only good idea he ever had was the one about pub signs. He became king by accident after his elder brother died of the plague, and his dad, the rightful heir to the throne upon the death of King Edward III, died of dysentery, and thus was not prepared for what life then through at him, with things going very badly very quickly indeed. This is perhaps partly because Richard was only 10 years old when they put that big, heavy crown on his head.

Historians, then, have long thought him to be completely insane, but this is largely down to Shakespeare's play, funnily enough called Richard II, that basically says he was a bit of a wild boy. This was probably not entirely true, but there was certainly something wrong with the king, demonstrated by the fact that he burnt down the family home after the death of his first wife and then, and this is the creepy bit, married Isabella of Valois, who was, in fact, a little girl who was only six years old at the time. Bear in mind that he was twenty-nine.

Finally removed from the throne by Henry Bolingbroke, who became King Henry IV, Richard was locked away in Pontefract Castle and promptly murdered a short time later on St Valentine's Day in 1400. Some say he actually starved to death, which is still murder when you think about it, but anyway, his body was taken down to London and put on display for all to see, which is odd, because Richard later turned up at Stirling Castle, where he lived for another 20 years. Dismissed by many as an imposter and described by nearly everyone as yet another lunatic, whoever was living at Stirling did nonetheless create lots of inconvenient rumours. As a result, the new king had the supposed body of Richard II exhumed from its remote burial place somewhere in rural Hertfordshire and re-interred in Westminster Abbey. Richard himself had prepared an elaborate tomb in the abbey, which already contained his first wife, and he finally joined her in 1413, though the rumours of his apparent survival did not cease fully until 1419, when whoever was living in Stirling Castle finally popped his clogs too.

Anyway, that's enough of kings, but before we go, it is worthwhile saying that Richard did not do too badly when it came to his death, assuming, of course, that he either starved to death or was swiftly dispatched with something very sharp. It could have been a lot worse, you see, and I am reminded here of perhaps my favourite death when it comes to monarchs, which is the case of King Edward II. Old Ed was a bit of a playboy and apparently preferred male company to female, so it is perhaps not surprising when his own wife had him murdered in a manner that suggested she did not approve of his antics, namely by having a red-hot poker thrust up his backside.

However, enough of that, as it is time to jump from the murderous middle-ages back to a more civilized time, that of the Romans. I suspect they never murdered each other with red-hot pokers, but then I guess you never really know what others get up to on a Saturday night, do you?

Just to the east of Bainbridge, you see, are the remains of an old Roman fort. These forts were much more common further north, towards Hadrian's Wall, for instance, so I was surprised to find out about Virosidum Roman Fort this far south, but you learn something every day when out exploring the countryside, I guess. If you want to see it, it's only a short walk away across the bridge and up the hill, where you will find it just behind the cemetery and which looks like a flat-topped hill, which is all that is basically left. You won't even need to risk getting shot by an irate farmer, as there is a public footpath across the field right next to it.

Anyway, Virosidum was originally occupied from the 2nd century. The Romans remained here until around the 5th century, when they all marched off, presumably back to Rome, I imagine. They may well have escaped on the old Roman road that ran from here to Ingleton across Cam Fell in a dead straight line, as Roman roads tend to do, of course, but what is amazing is that you can still follow the route of this road yourself as it is surprisingly well preserved and is now known as Cam High Road. The place was first excavated by a man called John Kirk, who came from none other than my home town of Hull, and by all accounts, he did a pretty good job, which is quite surprising as Kirk was, in fact, a doctor who also enjoyed dabbling in painting. Luckily perhaps, Kirk worked alongside another archaeologist named Robin Collingwood, who was in his lifetime the leading authority on Roman Britain, and it was he who came up with the idea that Hadrian's Wall was really nothing more than a sentry platform, which is something that is taken for granted nowadays but was revolutionary at the time. Anyway, Kirk and Collingwood managed to do a pretty good job between them, and they at least managed to begin serious excavations at Virosidum.

Much later, Kirk went on to found the York Castle Museum using much of his personal collection to get it going, and if you have ever been to this museum, you may well know that they have a recreation of a late Victorian street. What you may not know, however, is that this street is called Kirkgate directly in tribute to John Kirk, and as part of this work, he also managed to add museum curator to his long list of skills, working there for many years after that.

I somehow managed to drag Belle from her fireside spot, and as we went back outside, it was noticeably cooler, though not what I would call cold. Before we left Bainbridge, we went to inspect the village stocks, located just on the green not far from the Rose and Crown. They still looked in pretty good condition and would once have been used for punishing minor infringements of the law, such as public drunkenness, so I told Belle to be on her best behaviour. Victims would be locked into place for a few hours and subjected to the humiliation of any passers-by, who they may well have known personally, of course. Incidentally, the term laughing stock is often said to come from this, and while it might make sense, it is simply not true. Nonetheless, it's a good story, and the association between the term and the actual stocks has certainly grown over time, though once again, it really is not true.

And before we left the village completely, I took Belle for a splash in the river just a few yards south of the pub after crossing the bridge. There are a series of shallow waterfalls here, and despite the lateness of the day and the fairly cool temperature,

Belle was again straight in and splashing around in no time at all, much to the disgust of a couple of ducks that had themselves just been splashing about, until we arrived, that is. If you don't want to get wet, though, you can get a pretty good look at the falls from the bridge, but you can't beat a dog in some water for making you smile. I hoped that a side effect of this latest bath would be that she no longer smelt so bad, but for that, we would have to wait and see, or wait and smell, actually, when you think about it.

It was time to get a move on, and as is usually the case, we seemed to get back to the Herriot Way quicker than what it had taken us to get to the village. We were soon on Skellgill Lane and heading west, and after having had Belle on her lead for a while, I decided that not a lot of traffic used this road, so I let her off again. Obviously, as soon as I did this, a car came, so back on she went.

I knew we were on the right track when we passed a bed and breakfast called Luke's House, a name which had stuck in my head when I checked the map earlier because Robin, who of course would normally be walking alongside me if he wasn't such a pansy with his man-flu, has a son with the same name.

Shortly after Luke's House, we passed a small hamlet consisting of a farm, a bridge and a couple of guest houses, after which the road promptly stopped. I say a bridge, but I mean half a bridge, as it looked as if a recent passer-by had demolished most of it. I considered taking a picture and sending it to my wife along with a note asking if she had passed this way lately, but not wanting to die, I did not bother.

Through a gate and into a field, Belle was once again off and gone. There were some sheep very far off into the distance, but neither Belle nor I noticed them at first, as we were too busy sharing my sandwiches. I had brought some dog food along, but when I put the container down and took the lid off, she just looked at the biscuits I had so generously provided, apparently with a look of disgust on her face, and made no attempt to eat them. Instead, she licked her lips at my food, and I'm not sure if dogs normally eat ham, cheese and pickle sandwiches, but today at least, mine did.

She enjoyed it, too, so I gave her another one, as I was not all that hungry anyway. I then gave her some water, though she didn't want it, but then she had been drinking out of every stream, puddle and river we had come across, so she probably wasn't all that thirsty.

Although there were still no signs, this section of the way was much easier to follow. A wide and well-used farm track ran alongside a dry-stone wall, and there wasn't really any way to go wrong or get lost, not even for me.

Hills to our right blocked the view, but you could see clearly towards the south, which was on our left. The sun had been trying to come out, and visibility was good, so all in all, it was a remarkably good day considering the lateness of the year, yet there had still been hardly any people along the way. I was beginning to wonder if many people did this walk, and I was leaning heavily on probably not, at least not in late autumn, which is a shame because it is set in such truly beautiful countryside.

As easy as the path was to follow, it just seemed to go on and on for miles. I checked the map, and while we still seemed to have a long way to go, at least we were getting there. This was good, as I was certainly beginning to feel a bit tired, and I had noticed that Belle had slowed somewhat in her pace and was no longer tearing around and exploring everything along the way. Despite not having her lead on, she was walking directly behind me, and in her eyes, I knew she had had enough, and I felt a twinge of guilt running through me.

We stopped by a wall and shared the last of the sandwiches, and while we sat, I checked her paws. On one occasion many moons ago, when Belle was still more or less a puppy, I had taken her out on a very long run, at the end of which I discovered her feet were red-raw. She couldn't walk for a couple of days after that, and I felt as guilty as hell, so I wanted to avoid a repetition of that at all costs.

Thankfully, her feet were good, so after we shared the last of our food, which was a sausage roll, we plodded on. I told Belle that slow and steady wins the race, as we slowly tackled field after field, some with sheep and some without.

We passed through two farms that showed no signs of life whatsoever, but at the third, which was Litherskew, it was a hive of activity. Two people were washing a pair of red setters, which also appeared to be fond of rolling in brown stuff, apparently. A man worked on a tractor near them, while another carried a wheelbarrow around a barn. They all looked about as happy as Bambi when his mother was shot, and I include the humans in that as well.

I spoke to the couple washing the dogs who said they had been down to the river, and I presumed they meant the Ure. The dogs were actually being pretty good, especially when considering they were being washed with cold water from a hosepipe, though like I said, they looked more than a bit miserable, and I wondered what would unfold when I attempted to bathe Belle later on.

We moved on, following the path once more along the dry-stone wall, where the track soon took us onto a very nice tarmac road; however, I could tell that Belle did not like walking on it after all these miles. I walked on the grass, hoping she would follow me, and indeed she did, but I noticed she was even slower than before.

It was at this point that we passed more of the spaceships of the type we had seen near Helm, though we were a lot closer to these. Obviously not spaceships, the close proximity allowed me to see what they actually were, which was cattle feeders. Mystery solved.

We may have been walking a hundred yards or so south of

the actual route of the Herriot Way at this point. Still, I was not going to worry about such a small deviation and anyway, both routes converged at the same point on the outskirts of Sedbusk.

Upon checking the map, the actual route should take us through Sedbusk and onto Simonstone and Hardraw before looping back down to Hawes, but I honestly figured that Belle was really beginning to struggle. Combined with the fact that we were losing the light and starting to get cold, I decided that we would effectively finish at Sedbusk and walk down into Hawes. We could start next time exactly where we left off, which would, of course, mean adding a couple of miles next time, but for today, we were done.

We walked down into the town and straight back to the car, and when I opened the back door, Belle hauled herself onto the seat, and within seconds, she was asleep. She literally did not move for the next three hours, and when we got home, she had some food then jumped into her bed, where she slept for another twelve hours. I did the same, but not in her bed, of course, because that would just be silly.

THE HARD WORK

Hawes (nearly) to Keld (nearly)

We resumed our journey exactly where we had left off, at Sedbusk. It was now light, however, so we managed to get a good look at this pretty little village that had been shrouded in an inky darkness at the time of our last visit.

Rounding a bend to the village proper, up a slight hill, we found a small but pleasant village green surrounded by old stone houses, and a tiny dog of indiscernible type immediately ran up to Belle to sniff her butt. She wasn't too happy at this turn of events at such an early hour and issued a long, low growl in protest, and the playful little miscreant seemed to get the message as he bounced back to his owner.

Although it is indeed a very pretty little village, there appears to be not much going on. If you had been here in the summer of 1568, however, then you may well have caught a glimpse of Mary Queen of Scots as she passed through the place along the old drover's road on her way to her imprisonment at Bolton castle.

With nothing to keep us here today, we moved swiftly on, though I did exchange a brief good morning with the owner of the tiny devil dog that was still bouncing crazily around and which appeared to be as mad as a hatter. A finger post pointed us to the left and appeared to direct us straight through someone's garden, as indeed it did.

A narrow gate then led us into a small field full of sheep, so I put Belle back onto her lead which would also serve the purpose of controlling her for a short while, at least. On the first stage of this walk, Belle had been absolutely exhausted by the end of the day, and I put this partly down to the fact that, for the first few miles at least, she ran this way and that as I merely walked in a straight line, and she, therefore, must have walked at least twice as far as me, if not more.

This first field was tiny, and we crossed it in less than a minute, after which another narrow gate led us into the next, which was again full of sheep, and this pattern continued for countless tiny enclosures. Most had at least some sheep in them, so Belle stayed firmly attached to me, and although I was pretty sure that she would not chase or eat one of these little fluff balls, I didn't want to take the risk, as we must remember she is a bit of wild one at times.

My knees and legs were somewhat painful this morning, and I was hoping I would be able to walk it off. It was nothing to do with walking that had caused it, however, but it was due to a party I had been to a couple of days before. It was the parents' party for my son's football team, and we had been to a dinner dance, although I am not necessarily renowned as the world's greatest dancer, and I am rarely seen in such activities, it should be noted. However, after a few pints of beer and several Jäger-bombs, I become John Travolta, apparently, which rather explains the pain I am feeling in my knees today.

My wife was also a bit angry with me for another reason at the party. She had asked me if I had been embarrassed when I repeatedly went back to the buffet to get more cake, as in the end, I had about four or five servings. I told her that I had not been embarrassed at all, as every time I went back, I explained to the server that each piece was for my wife. I don't think she was very impressed.

I lost count of how many gates we had passed through after about a dozen or so, and after walking through a small farm where it was not sheep on the menu but chickens, followed by several derelict looking barns, we came to a working farm that had a rather troublesome style to get over.

It was high, around five feet or so, and was made up of a few steps on either side with a flat platform at the top. Although there was a wide metal gate next to it, this was firmly locked. There was no option, then, but to tackle the style, although I knew before I even attempted it that there would be no way Belle could get over unaided.

I climbed over it and then encouraged Belle to follow, but the steps were too steep. She looked at the gate instead, trying to find a way through, but there was none, so when she returned to the style's steps, I once more encouraged her up.

She struggled up in a somewhat unladylike manner, but then she is getting a bit old, and managed to get to the next-but-last step, whereby I had to grab her collar and help her onto the top. She looked around her, and she was at the same height as my head now, and I knew there was no way she would walk down the steps by herself, or if she did, she might hurt herself, as five feet is a long jump down for an old dog like Belle.

I dropped my rucksack to the ground as I realized that I would have to lift her down myself, but even as I went in to get her, I could see that she wasn't entirely sure about the situation and was far from happy. Nonetheless, I grabbed hold of her in a sort of tight cuddle and slowly lowered her to the ground, placing her gently down, at which point she ran off straight away.

It is important to say at this stage that we had just been through several sheep fields, and sheep tend to poop a lot. Belle is not all that bothered about what she steps in, and indeed she had probably already been rolling in something brown and sticky as well, so once she had run off, and I glanced at my jacket, I realized that everything she had previously been in contact with was now smeared all over me. On a positive note, if I now fell directly onto a rather large and fresh cowpat, it probably wouldn't make much difference, as I was already filthy, so I simply shrugged my shoulders, put my rucksack back on, and carried on.

We were at Simonstone, a tiny hamlet on the way to Hardraw, and after a quick glance at the map and a bit of confusion as to which way the path went, I realized we would have to cross the road and head through the grounds of the Simonstone Hotel. Although technically I did get lost for just a moment or ten, I always say that I'm not, in fact, lost, I'm just exploring, which is pretty much true when you think about it.

The hotel looked very upmarket, and as I held on to the muddy lead attached to my also muddy dog, I dared not venture in. They do afternoon teas and luxury weekend breaks and the like, so I did not think they would appreciate one muddy man and his rather damp dog leaving a trail of scruffy footprints and, in the dog's case, at least, muddy paw-prints, across their nice shiny lobby.

Before we walked by completely, however, I noticed a small plaque on a short pole and, presuming it to be a menu, wandered over to have a look, although it did seem to be an odd place to put a menu, which was just outside of the wall and next to the drive.

What we found was like striking gold. The plaque read as follows:

Here lies the BBC career of Jeremy Clarkson who had a fracas on this spot 4th March 2015. The rest is legend.

I think Belle was as numb struck as me. I was, of course, familiar with the story surrounding Mr Clarkson, which tells of what went on late one night at some hotel somewhere, but I had no idea that the place was anywhere around here. I had to agree with the small sign, however, that the rest is indeed legend, although, for those not in the know, it went as follows.

After a long day of filming Top Gear in the area, the production team and crew arrived back at the hotel, which was, of course, this one, the Simonstone. Mr Clarkson, or Jezza to his wives and girlfriends, had ordered a steak, which had in fact been ready for the agreed time of 7.30pm.

It is perhaps unfortunate then that it was nearer 11pm by the time everyone rolled into the hotel. As might be expected, the chefs had departed many hours before, and staff had long since thrown away Jezza's by-now somewhat crispy steak and had prepared a cold platter instead. The platter was, apparently, very nice indeed and was incredibly well prepared. However, there was just one problem, in that it was not a nice big juicy steak.

It was unlucky then, for Clarkson's producer Oisin Tymon, that it was he who had to break the bad news to Jeremy about his unfortunate steak and its cold and rather insubstantial meaty replacement. Mr Clarkson didn't take too kindly to this, and for some reason, possibly relating to the exhaustion of a long day filming, he gave Tymon a good slap. Unfortunately, he also commented on Tymon's heritage, suggested he was lazy and is said to have called him a rather nasty word.

Ultimately, Clarkson no longer works for the BBC, but I hear he is nonetheless doing rather well running a farm somewhere in the Cotswolds and also has a bit of a side gig going on with the largest streaming company on the planet. In the meantime, Top Gear has gone on to have rather a lot of presenters and, well, let's just leave it at that.

And in a final twist, the hotel manager has recently announced commemorative steak nights to remember these infamous events. Don't arrive too late, though, as if you do, you might well be served with a cold platter and a slap across the face.

At the other side of the hotel, then, we encountered another one of those extremely narrow gates that are intended to stop sheep and annoy chubby hikers. Once the gate was open, there was the additional obstacle of a squeeze between the stones of the wall, and this one proved to be very problematic indeed, being possibly the narrowest we had encountered so far.

I opened the gate and told Belle to go through, which she tried to do, but unfortunately, her big fat backside was, well, too big. I had a little chuckle as I watched her once or twice until she gave up completely, turned around and then wandered off.

Glancing around, there seemed no other obvious way for us to go, and the wall certainly looked too high to lift her over, so I had no option but to open the gate once again and give her a second try.

Again, she squeezed and twisted to no avail, but then on the third or fourth attempt, she managed to somehow get through, popping out on the other side into a big muddy puddle. She wasn't bothered about the soaking whatsoever and simply ran off to chase a squirrel.

I followed her through, in somewhat the same manner as Belle, it has to be said, and it occurred to me that these gates and squeezes were quite possibly designed for stick insects.

The path then led us diagonally across a field to yet another squeeze, which was thankfully not as severe as the last, before leading us to a farm.

Whoever lived here was very creative, as on the outside wall was a walking-stick shop. There were dozens of them, all stacked up neatly in various styles, sizes, and colours, and they were on sale for the bargain price of only three pounds each. I briefly considered getting one as a souvenir but soon dismissed the idea, a decision that would come back to haunt me much later in the day.

Somewhere from on our right came the sound of rushing water, lots of it apparently, and this was presumably Hardraw Beck, soon to be our first stop of the day. To get there, though, we would have to go down into the village and through a pub, a sacrifice I would happily take for the team, as the waterfall was privately owned, and that was the only way in.

The path became quite steep as it led us down into the village, and I thought it best to let Belle off the lead so I wouldn't drag her to her grave when I inevitably slipped and fell to my muddy death, leaving her an orphan dog to survive out here in the wilderness all alone. However, I reckoned that if I did, she probably wouldn't last two minutes, being the city dog that she is.

The views down to the village and beyond were fantastic, even on a day like today, which was grey and gloomy, with a patchwork of fields spreading to the wild hills in the distance, and the tiles of the houses below us resembling one of those incredibly fiendish jigsaws where all the bits look the same.

I didn't slip to my death, luckily, but I did manage to cover my bum in yet more of England's finest mud at some point or another on the way down. This left me damp and cold, but at least I was still alive, whereas Belle didn't miss a single step. I guess that's the benefit of having four-wheel drive, if you know what I mean.

Safely down at the bottom, and I mean the bottom of the hill, not my bottom, Belle was once again back on her lead as we slipped through yet another gate and into the tiny village of Hardraw.

The village is perhaps famous for one thing, and one thing only: the waterfall that bears its name. Quite wonderfully, perhaps, Hardraw force is located along the beck of the same name, deep within a ravine, though it is actually just outside of Hardraw village itself. The beck, by the way, flows south from here for just a few hundred feet more before it enters the River Ure that we had followed on and off during our journey through Wensleydale.

We came out right next to the Green Dragon Inn, which was exactly where we wanted to be, and after taking a quick photo of the pub, which was very pretty with its ivy-clad walls and Georgian windows, we ventured around to find the entrance to the waterfall.

I had known that there was a small fee to pay as the waterfall is located on private land. Still, it was only a few pounds, and besides, we could also visit the Green Dragon Inn, an excellent and traditional 13th-century pub featuring open fires, beamed ceilings and stone walls, or so I had heard. There is no way I was missing out on that, so I decided to check out the pub first. I just hoped they were dog friendly.

Going in, it wasn't a disappointment, and after getting lost in the various nooks and crannies while I searched for the toilets, I finally found the bar where many of the names of the beers on offer were already somewhat familiar to me, as they will be to you, too, after reading these pages. Semerwater Pale Ale was on offer from the Wensleydale Brewery, as was Butter Tubs Bitter from Askrigg, among others, and it took me some time before I finally decided on the Semerwater. I would have to come back, I promised myself, to try the others. Belle just wanted normal water.

The Green Dragon also has a brand-new claim to fame. Although the original Drover's Arms in the first television series of *All Creatures Great and Small* was actually the King's Arms back at Askrigg, which we passed through earlier, of course, and the new series of the television show uses exterior shots of *The Devonshire* public house in Grassington, the interior shots of the pub for the new series are actually shot right here, at the *Green Dragon.*

And then there is the waterfall, which is said to be the highest in England, at around 100 feet from top to bottom, but to be honest, there are quite a few caveats to add to that. Technically, it is the highest unbroken, above-ground waterfall in England most of the time, and furthermore, there is now some debate as to whether the waterfall can still be considered to be a natural feature due to some work that was done to it a while back.

It's only fair to mention all of this, and I will let you decide on the various claims made about the waterfall, so here we go.

First of all, the nearby waterfall at Gaping Gill, a large underground cavern, dwarfs Hardraw by a factor of three, being around 300 feet unbroken from top to bottom, but it is, of course, underground. Secondly, Malham Cove, a large limestone cliff that was previously a waterfall thousands of years ago, temporarily regained its place as England's highest waterfall in 2015, after Storm Desmond once again saw water briefly running over the top of it before plummeting around 230 feet to the stream below.

And lastly, a flood in 1899 over the top of Hardraw was so powerful it destroyed the lip of the waterfall. The resulting torrent then ravaged homes and building downstream and even uprooted bodies from the graveyard at St Mary and St John's Church, which must have been a bit of a sight to see. Repair work was subsequently carried out by the then owner of the land, Lord Wharton, and the lip was reconstructed and is now pinned together, hence the debate on whether or not it can still be considered a natural formation, though I think on reflection, the answer is yes.

Regardless, Hardraw Force is incredibly popular with visitors, and both Turner and Wordsworth visited the falls and painted them, and in fact, stayed right here at the Green Dragon Inn. And if the waterfall looks familiar when you get here, well, you may have seen it in the movies, as this is where Maid Marion ogled a naked Kevin Costner as Robin Hood in Prince of Thieves, the filthy girl.

And the waterfall is actually part of a series called the Yoredale Series, and if you remember, Yoredale is the old name for Wensleydale. Beware, however, as this is yet another place that is supposedly haunted. In years gone by, three friends fell out while visiting the waterfall and ended up fighting, resulting in the deaths of one of them. If you come here during a thunderstorm then, you may well hear his cries in between the claps of thunder, so don't say you haven't been warned.

Furthermore, a rather famous fossil was found here in the

late 1970s, that of the footprints of a megapezia, with the best way to describe it being some kind of evolving sea creature that is exploring the land, one of the first examples of its kind apparently, and representing the period of evolution when the fishes finally became sick and tired of being eaten by sharks and decided to move house to somewhere a bit drier and with nicer neighbours. It is estimated to be 340 million years old, which is, curiously enough, the same age that my kids think I am. They once even tried to have me carbon dated. You might think I'm being a bit paranoid, but I never trust kids anyway. Think about it – they're here to replace us.

As for paying to get in, I have heard a lot of negative comments on this, but the present owners, Mark and Yvonne, have stated their case very clearly, according to their website at least, in that the paths, bridges and walkways of the waterfall require constant upkeep at substantial cost, so what is a few pounds really?

Anyway, after a quick look in the pub, I soon found the entrance to the falls. I had expected a small shed or perhaps a shack, but this was a full-on visitor centre with what looked like a café or restaurant attached, although that part of it did not appear to be open today. I wandered in and found the inside as well designed as the outside, and an older man was talking to a slightly younger man behind the counter.

I waited patiently, not wanting to interrupt as they finished their conversation, and after just a few seconds, the man behind the counter asked if he could help me. Rather than tell him the truth, and admit that I am beyond help, I replied that yes, he could. I paid for my ticket, gleefully accepted my free map like an excited child (well, who doesn't like free stuff?) and passed through the turnstile to go and see the waterfall.

Belle was a bit stumped by the turnstile and seemed to be slightly reluctant to follow me through. I imagine this was a common problem, as on the other side was a box of dog biscuits which the man behind the counter said was there for just this purpose. Sure enough, as soon as I waved a small brown meaty thing around, Belle was straight through.

I was conscious of the time, as we had a lot of walking to do today. The fact that we had finished early last time added at least a couple of miles onto today, yet I really wanted to include this waterfall in our walk as well. I had decided, therefore, that we would just go there and back to have a look and not waste any unnecessary time, although, in all honesty, I reckon we could easily have spent an hour or two here exploring the lovely woodlands that bounded both sides of the river.

As we came out of the visitor centre, I was thrilled to see a red squirrel hopping along the fence to my right, though luckily, Belle missed it, or she would probably have chased off after it. She can't help it, as she is a prisoner of her chase instinct. In her time, she has indeed chased many squirrels up various trees near our home more times than I can remember. However, they were all of the common grey and invasive example of the species and not our own native red type.

The grey squirrel, of course, was introduced from America in the late 1800s, and due to a combination of it stealing food from the smaller native red, as well as the introduction of the pox virus, which kills red squirrels but not grey ones, the red is now critically endangered in most of the country. However, pockets of them do still exist, and we are lucky to find ourselves in one today

So, who is responsible for this disaster? Well, don't believe anyone who tells you that it is impossible to say. Recent genetic testing by Imperial College London has shown that most wild squirrels in the country today are genetically related to a batch released at Woburn Abbey in the 1880s by an idiot called Herbrand Russell. We should have known, really, because what type of name is Herbrand? And if I have offended anyone out there called Herbrand, please can I give you a bit of advice? Get a new name.

Anyway, good old Herbrand, or Dick to his mates, probably, was the 11th Duke of Bedford, and his picture shows him to be as pompous as he sounds. With a ridiculously manicured moustache, he was actually the President of the Zoological Society of London for almost forty years, which is somewhat ironic considering the damage he did to the British countryside.

He went to great lengths not to pay tax and hid for much of his life on his vast estate, probably counting his bloody squirrels. Indeed, his own grandson, Ian Russell, a much better name I have to admit, was even quoted of saying of his grandad, '*A selfish, forbidding man . . . he lived a cold, aloof existence, isolated from the outside world by a mass of servants, sycophants and an eleven-mile wall.*' That says all we need to know, doesn't it?

Because of the critical state that the red squirrel is now in, there have been moves for some years to try to reduce the number of greys, and unfortunately, if you want reds to thrive, you have to kill greys, at least according to several experts in the field. I know grey squirrels are cute but don't have a go at me; I'm just the messenger.

Anyway, after the war, members of the public were encouraged to shoot them and were paid a shilling for every grey tail they handed in. When guns went out of fashion, the Forestry Commission tried poisoning them with warfarin, a blood thinner, which did nothing to solve the squirrel problem but did kill tens of thousands of other animals in the process.

There may be light at the end of the tunnel, though. And the answer is simpler than anyone had thought it would be. That answer is the reintroduction of pine martens to our forests, which have until now only managed to cling on in parts of Scotland.

Now, while pine martens are certainly not racist and will happily eat squirrels of any colour, they tend to eat more grey ones than red. This is because grey ones are stupid. They really are, and when a grey squirrel sees a pine marten, it does not see it as a threat, as pine martens have never lived in the parts of America where squirrels live.

Some squirrels even approach the pine martens, maybe wanting to play or out of curiosity, or perhaps just wondering what the hell they are, so they are presumably somewhat surprised when they then have their heads bitten clean off.

Anyway, red squirrels have evolved to recognize pine martens for what they are, which is vicious, cold-blooded killers, so as soon as they catch a scent of one, they are off. This explains why red squirrels are hanging on in Scotland, where the pine marten is still relatively common, so their reintroduction to the rest of the country could well be the answer.

This reintroduction has already begun, with a small population now in England and Wales, and the eventual hope is to rebalance the ecosystem. In England, this has happened in Gloucestershire in the Forest of Dean, and those in charge have specifically mentioned the grey squirrel as one of the reasons for their reintroduction. If nature takes its course, the red squirrel may well be saved yet.

It really was only a short walk to the waterfall itself, and it was indeed worth every penny to see it, and I even managed to get a half-decent photo of Belle sitting in front of it. I had a quick look around myself, half tempted as I was to climb the fence for a better look until I saw the *no-entry* signs, though being a bit of a chicken, I changed my mind.

Photo in hand, we ventured back to the visitor centre to continue our walk, and although we had been no more than fifteen minutes or so, I was still adamant that it had been worth both the time and the money.

I found a tree on the way back that really stuck out, as someone had carved on it how much Gary loved Clare. Whenever I see trees engraved like this, I have to be honest and say that I don't find it remotely cute or romantic. In fact, it just alarms me that so many people take knives with them on dates.

When we got back to the visitor centre, I had a long chat with the gentleman who served us. It turned out that he was the owner, Mark, and he clearly loved the place. He spoke about the work he had put in over the years and the countless hours he had spent showing people around and was clearly a man who was very happy with his place in life.

As for the cost to get in, I can once again definitely say it was worth it, and Belle agreed, judging by all the fun she had in the water, though she didn't actually have to pay, of course.

It was, however, time to move on. We still had to make up what ground we had lost by finishing early last time, and we wouldn't really start today's walk, so to speak, until we got to Hawes, which was still another couple of miles away, so with a final goodbye to Mark, Belle and I wandered off once and for all.

We found our path almost opposite the pub, which after a couple more squeeze gates, led us into meadows and fields full of yet more sheep. The path was a good one, easy to follow at this stage, fairly straight, and was, at least for a while, made of sturdy flagstones. However, these soon gave way to a muddy track, where I bumped into a lady walking her dog, and it dawned on me that she was the first person we had met along the path today. She was very chatty and was called Angie, she said, and I actually mean that the first thing she told me was that she was very chatty and Angie was her name.

Her dog was some type of Collie. As she and Belle took turns to sniff each other, chatty Angie told me about the holiday she was currently enjoying up here. She had come from Hawes, she explained, which is where her motorhome was, and was doing a circular walk today as she did not fancy driving the thing along the tiny roads that were the only option if you wanted to come to nice places such as Hardraw. I understood what she meant, as it was bad enough in a car, and there is no way I would want to drive anything bigger up here either.

She went on to tell me about the weather that she had enjoyed over the last few days, although enjoyed is perhaps not the best word she could have used as it had been, quite frankly, terrible. We spoke for a bit, and I told her what we were doing and how we intended to cross Great Shunner Fell later that day, to which she replied that most of the snow was probably gone by now anyway.

I stopped her and enquired about this snow of which she spoke, and she replied that, oh yes, if I had been here just a few days before, I would have been knee-deep in snow. I must admit that I had not considered this a possibility, and although I had brought waterproofs, I had not really counted on snow and all the problems that it can bring us merry walkers and our meagre city dogs.

Snow, you see, will slow you down. It will make you slip and slide and somehow make you both hot and cold simultaneously. Hot when you struggle through it, you see, often up a steep and cruel hill, and cold when it inevitably gets into your boots or shoes or when your gloves get damp as you ultimately give in and start to make snow-balls like all the other big kids.

We finished our conversation with goodbye and good luck, and each moved off in our respective directions, them towards Hardraw and us towards Hawes. Chatty Angie had lived up to her name, and we had been talking for about a quarter of an hour, but I had enjoyed every minute of it, though it now really was time to move on.

The path remained clear and fairly straight, and as we passed through field after field, slowly but surely plodding along, the occasional sheep gave us a curious glance, and the odd pheasant cackled noisily as we passed. I don't think Belle knew what was making the noise, however. As I watched her ears prick up with the sound, she looked decidedly on edge and appeared to be glancing all around her in search of whatever strange beast that might possibly be about to spring out of the bushes next.

Belle finally found a pheasant in the next field, and I saw her sniffing at it from a distance. Of course, at the time, I could not see that it was a pheasant, or more accurately a dead pheasant, so I was not initially alarmed when she started rolling around in it, as filthy dogs tend to do from time to time.

However, when I caught up with her and saw what she had done, I was speechless. The bird had clearly been dead for some time. It had most certainly started the decomposition process, but let's just say it was still somewhat in the early stages of the journey. Entrails were bright and colourful, and there looked as if there might be some meat on the bones for anything that was not too discerning about what it ate, but the thing that struck me most was the smell. There was a definite stink of rotting meat, and all I could think of was what Belle would smell like when she was back in the car later on. She might have to walk home, I figured. It's only a hundred miles or so.

The path we were on was actually the Pennine Way, which we would be jumping on and off today by the way, and as we had left Hardraw, we had passed close to Hardraw Beck. After a mile of walking east, we had again encountered the same water that had zigged and zagged through the fields to our south, but it had now changed its name to the River Ure, and which Hardraw Beck had become a part of just south of the village.

The path spat us out onto a minor road that would take us down into Hawes itself, and after having had to stop for a couple of passing cars, we were soon hopping over the old railway bridge into the pretty little market town. Just to the left of the bridge, I noticed a train parked up on a platform, which is odd because I had read that the Wensleydale Railway had ceased running many moons ago, but it turns out that the train is actually a part of the Wensleydale Museum.

The museum wouldn't be here today if it had not been for a local artist, Marie Hartley, and her friend, writer Ella Ponte-fract, who worked incredibly hard for many years with the sole purpose being to ensure that artefacts and records detailing historic life in the Yorkshire Dales remained right here where they belonged. The pair also wrote many books describing life in the dales and would have written many more if Ella had not died prematurely early in 1945 of complications of high blood pressure, something that was sadly untreatable at the time.

Following Ella's tragic death, Marie was then helped by Joan Ingleby, and together they carried on recording life in the dales, therefore continuing the job of making a permanent record of a way of life that was quickly vanishing as the modern world slowly but surely encroached upon these beautiful hills and dales.

Marie and Joan also wrote books, twenty-two in all, which again told of the old ways of life in these very dales, and which became very popular, at least for a while. People would visit their home, Coles House, back at Askrigg, which they had by then turned into an unofficial museum. It was there that visitors would presumably gaze in wonder at such oddities as packhorse collars, bridal jugs, and rather a lot of knitting needles.

When the collection became too big for their house and their barn was also full to the rafters, they finally decided to look for a more permanent home for their beloved treasures. So it was here at the old railway station where, in the late 1970s, the Dales Countryside Museum came into being, housing the vast collection of treasures gathered by Pontefract, Hartley and Ingleby, and which is where it remains to this very day.

Lastly on this, Hartley and Pontefract also became quite famous for something else. In the 1930s, and while they were on their travels scouring these hills and dales for antique knitting needles, farming implements and anything else they could get their hands on, they reputedly found a feral child living wild and alone in the ruins of a farmhouse high in the hills above Keld, but that is another story altogether and one that we will go into that a little further on in our walk, as for now, it is time to move on.

We soon came to what looked to be the main street, where I was delighted to find a small sculpture that I had wanted to see for some time. Although you cannot tell by looking, this sculpture has been something of a talking point in Hawes in recent years, and it sparked a bit of a scandal, or more accurately, it did so in the eyes of one resident at least.

It looks pretty harmless, and indeed it is. Standing at around 7-feet tall, this sculpture features a dapper-looking farmer and his trusty sheepdog, along with a sheep, of course. Perfectly innocent, you may say, and you would be right.

But wait a minute. What is that in the shepherd's mouth? Well, it is a humble smoking pipe, and that is exactly what caused the problem, apparently. One local resident, who I shall not name, had a bit of a fit about as soon as she heard about these proposals, insisting it would send the wrong message to the children about smoking. She objected to the erection in the strongest terms, arguing it would damage the reputation of Hawes particularly and the Yorkshire Dales National Park in general and would send the place to the bowels of hell for this clearly and obviously heinous act. I'm actually making that bit up, of course, but you know what I mean. Furthermore, our mystery complainant suggested that because the sculpture is opposite the doctor's surgery, it might even give visitors to the town the wrong impression, whatever that means.

Luckily, the local council completely ignored her, presumably telling her to shove her own pipe somewhere that the sun didn't shine and refused to believe her when she claimed lots of other people had also commented on this dastardly sculpture, and they ultimately granted permission for it to be put in place, right opposite the doctor's surgery.

And the best bit about this little story? Well, it turns out that the sculpture was provided, free of charge, by someone called Glen, Lord Lincoln, who had evidently quite enjoyed his little holiday to Hawes some time back and wanted to give the town a small gift in return.

Actually, that turns out not to be the best bit at all, for what I found out next had me flabbergasted while simultaneously howling with laughter. It turns out that none other than our local busybody had once written a rather dry-sounding book called something like *boring ropemakers of Hawes past and present*, and what was on the cover of this book? Why, it was her husband, of course. And what does he have in his mouth? Well, that would be a pipe, wouldn't it? There's nothing like a little bit of hypocrisy, is there?

In fairness to her, many good things can be said about this particularly busy resident, and although she was clearly on the wrong side of the argument when it came to the sculpture incident, she is nonetheless a very well-liked member of the local community. She was an integral part of the battle to save the Settle to Carlisle Railway in 1989, and she is now a very vocal part of the campaign to fully reopen the Wensleydale Railway. She has also made the rope-making business a qualified success, giving many people in the town much-needed jobs.

Hawes itself proves to be very nice and nothing like the bowels of hell. We followed a small street called Town Foot, where I discovered that the old school is now a Funky Pheasant, whatever that was, and there were lots of small shops for the weary tourist to shelter in should it rain, which it was now trying to do. It is a bustling little village, and we are lucky to arrive here on market day, and I soon noticed Belle eyeing up various pork pies, sausage rolls, and countless other pastries spread before us on a rather large stall. When she started to lick her lips, I gave in and bought us both a small treat to enjoy before we set off once more.

I should probably already have known it was market day, as when we drove through Hawes on the way to Sedbergh this morning, we had to pull the car to the side of the road due to being met by around a million sheep coming from the opposite direction. It had been a strange sight for us city-dwellers, but I had rather enjoyed the encounter, and Belle certainly had. She had spent the entire time looking through the car window licking her lips and thinking of Sunday dinners, probably, and she had been absolutely entranced by what she had seen.

Hawes is actually a town rather than a village and is said to be one of the highest market towns in the country, apparently, although there is no way to tell this by looking around. The name, by the way, means a pass between the mountains, something that can be demonstrated by simply looking around, with high hills disappearing into the clouds around us in all directions.

Belle enjoyed her sausage roll immensely, or so I presumed, based on the fact that she swallowed it whole, more or less. I was still eating mine as we crossed the road towards the church, and as Belle looked jealously at my half-finished pastry, I thought I had better finish it quickly before she got any funny ideas.

St Margaret's church is pretty impressive, and by English standards anyway, is relatively recent, having only been built in the mid-1800s. Before that, the town had been tiny, but rapid expansion resulted in the need for a much bigger church. Architects were consulted, and although what stands before us is, as I have already said, very nice indeed, Hawes, unfortunately, missed out on something that could have been absolutely spectacular.

The reason for this, you see, is that one of the unsuccessful designs had been drawn up by none other than George Edmund Street, more commonly known as G.E. Street, who went on to become one of the most famous and influential architects of the Victorian age. To give you an idea of his importance, his most famous work is probably the Royal Courts of Justice in London, although he also designed many buildings right across the country, including churches, schools, and private homes, among many others. His style was classic Victorian Gothic, which means really fancy if truth be told, and while St Margarets is all very nice, it could have been much, well, nicer.

We wandered around the churchyard, and I was surprised to look at my map only to discover that we were once again on the Pennine Way, which ran straight through it. I followed the path to the burial grounds, as there was something I wanted to see, which was a memorial to a terrible train crash that had happened nearby many years ago. The memorial was in the form of a cross, and I soon found it under a tree. For one awful second, I thought Belle was going to pee on it, but luckily, she changed her mind and used the tree instead.

The tragedy had happened at Hawes Junction in 1910, and a dozen people had been killed, with many more injured.

I had heard about the crash while out walking many moons ago, after coming across the chimney of one of the trains that had been involved. It had been found near to Garsdale station in the 1980s, and after initially puzzling everyone as to its origins, someone finally noticed a photograph of one of the trains involved in the Hawes Junction crash, where the train that had been involved could clearly be seen missing its chimney. A quick forensic examination by almost everyone soon decided that it definitely was what all had presumed it to be, and the chimney has been on display ever since, though it was moved to Ribblehead railway station in 2018, which is where I first saw it.

The crash was a bad one, even for the standards of the time. That era regularly saw several fatal crashes almost every year, though, for some reason, 1910 was even worse than most.

It had happened on Christmas Eve, early in the morning, and all those involved stated that it was incredibly bad weather that day. Strong winds howled around the hills, and rain battered against windows, and of course, the shortness of the day at that time of year meant that it was pitch black outside.

It was nearing the end of a long ten-hour shift for signalman Alfred Sutton when a perfect storm of events began to build, and indeed, he had already been joined by his relief, a man called

Simpson. Sutton had halted two light engines, driven by men called Scott and Bath, both of which had been heading for Carlisle, intending to let the faster St Pancras to Glasgow express train pass first. After this had passed, Sutton would release the line for the slower and smaller trains to resume their journey.

Unfortunately, the express was delayed, and while Sutton dealt with a very busy section of track, he somehow forgot about the two smaller trains. With the express finally on his section of the line, he inadvertently changed all of the signals to go, and the drivers of the two smaller engines presumed the signal was for them. They trundled off at around twenty-five miles-per-hour, totally unaware that they were now in front of a large and fast express train weighing many hundreds of tons, travelling at sixty miles-per-hour and still accelerating.

The two smaller trains passed through a tunnel at Moorcock, and it was only when one of the drivers happened to glance back that he saw the lights of the express approaching rapidly from behind. At the same time, the express driver saw the signal lights on the back of the smaller engine ahead of him, and he applied his emergency break almost immediately.

It was already too late, however. The braking system on the trains in those days took almost four seconds to fully engage, whereas the time from initial sighting to impact was estimated to be only six seconds anyway, so braking had little effect. The accident investigation report describes what happened next in technical terms, stating that the rear train *overtook* the two smaller engines, but what this actually means is that the express crashed into the back of them and more or less smashed straight through them, which makes this use of the word *overtook* interesting in the extreme.

Although I have been describing them as smaller engines, they had been coupled together and between them weighed around a hundred tons, and were of course comprised of lots of heavy, thick pieces of metal, much of which was very hot, and both of which contained a couple of very powerful fires, so it was really a case of lots of very substantial metal machines all colliding and smashing together in a deadly, fiery inferno.

The report also goes on to describe what happened to the passenger carriages as *telescoping*, which again is perhaps the most inventive use of the word that I have ever come across. What it actually means is that one train carriage completely crashed through the other one in the same way that sections of a telescope fit inside one another. Bear in mind that all of these trains were full of passengers, so this kind of encounter was simply deadly.

Twelve people died in this terrible tragedy, all of whom had been sat in the first two carriages. Many probably did not die instantly, however, so what happened next is possibly even worse.

The doors on the carriages had been locked at the time, so people had difficulty escaping. Many people lay injured in the wreckage, although they were too injured to move anyway, so this was perhaps a moot point. Anyway, the onboard lights in some of these carriages had been powered by gas, and when the impact happened, the gas lines were ruptured, and gas immediately began to leak. The report states that all of the gas escaped within just a few minutes and ignited. Therefore, it is highly likely that some passengers died from this terrible aspect of the disaster and not the crash itself. This was further compounded by the fact that, at the time, most of the passenger carriages were made of wood and also contained highly flammable upholstery, which only served to fan the flames even further.

The express was derailed and left on its side, having gouged through the side of the railway cutting as it slowed. The wreckage of the two smaller engines came to rest a couple of hundred yards in front of the express train, such was the force of the impact. Behind all of this, around 400 yards of track had been completely ripped up and destroyed as the impact had occurred. It was truly an epic disaster that made national headlines in all of the newspapers, and it was particularly poignant because it had happened on Christmas Eve with all of those on board trying to get home to see their loved ones.

Ultimately, it was decided that human error was the chief cause of the accident, with all fingers pointing, not surprisingly, at Signalman Sutton for much of the blame. In fairness, the report pointed out that Sutton had been at the end of a very long shift and had extra traffic to deal with since it was Christmas Eve. On top of this, though, it was found that Scott and Bath, the drivers of the two smaller engines, had failed to obey something called *Rule 55*, which is meant to make it impossible for trains to be forgotten like this. *Rule 55* states that after standing still for two or three minutes at the most, drivers should sound their whistle, and after five minutes, one of the firemen should have returned to the signal box to remind Sutton of their position. They failed to do this for around twenty minutes, probably because it was cold and wet outside.

Sutton realized his enormous mistake just moments after the point of no return, and he is reported to have told his relief man, Simpson, to *go tell the station master that I am afraid I have wrecked the Scotch Express.*

Some good did ultimately come from this crash, though, it must be said. The man in charge of the accident report, Major John Pringle, recommended that the lighting systems used on trains should be electrified and that track circuits should be installed at Hawes Junction and all other similar locations with heavy traffic. Track circuits are basically electrical devices that show whether or not a track is occupied, and are cheap and simple to install, having been available since the 1870s, and could have worked towards preventing this and many other disasters. While this is interesting, I also found out from the accident report that at the time, all of these investigations were carried out by men from the army, and in particular and perhaps not surprisingly, from the Royal Engineers.

I had had enough of death and accidents, however, and decided it was time to cheer myself up, so I took Belle mouse hunting in the church. Don't panic; there's no need to call the authorities, as it is wooden mice that we seek. The church, you see, contains many pieces of furniture built by a man called Robert Thompson, a Yorkshire native who eventually gained the name *Mouseman* due to the carvings he added to his furniture.

However, it was not just mice that Thompson carved. He also left behind some beautiful and quite intricate carvings that included local flora and fauna, religious symbols, and even a mediaeval-style green man. I had not come across the green man before, but it is thought that it symbolises the cycle of life, death and rebirth, though there is also speculation that it is meant to bridge the gap between pagan and Christian beliefs. This is partly because the sites of many churches that contain green man carvings were previously pagan sacred places, but this is all really just speculation.

There is nobody in the church when I peek my head around the door, so I take Belle in, although I am not really sure if dogs are allowed in churches. There is no sign forbidding them, which I take as a doggy welcome.

She is very well behaved and does not try to make her mark on anything, but I keep an eye on her anyway. Looking around the church, I struggled to find a mouse on any of the furniture for what seemed like an age, but when I found one on a pew, I immediately found another, and after that, I was on a roll.

There is also a strange coffin cart in the church, I discover. Its proper name is a bier, and this one looked pretty old yet was in great condition. Resisting the temptation to lie down on it and take a selfie, I moved on.

We crossed over a bridge, below which was a small but impressive stream complete with a very pretty waterfall. I stopped to take a picture and noticed that you could rent one of the stone cottages overlooking it, which would surely be a wonderful place to spend a weekend or even longer. I suspected that many buildings in the town were now available through companies such as Airbnb, with many houses now beyond the reach of youngsters in pretty little towns such as this. Don't get me wrong, I think it's great that you can rent a cottage directly from the owner, and Airbnb is certainly an interesting invention. I had read a while back that you could even rent out a small country if you so desired, assuming, of course, you had buckets of cash available. For a mere $70,000 a night, the whole of Liechtenstein could be yours, and even though it's only a small country, it would probably have room for you and nine hundred of your besties. No good for me, though, as I don't even know a hundred people, never mind nine hundred.

Walking down the high street, many shoppers were milling about and gazing in shop windows, including lots of ladies, which got me thinking.

Whenever Belle goes up to a young lady while we are out, you see, I have found the perfect way of putting sheer terror into them, and even more so, into their husbands and boyfriends. I generally wait until Belle has nuzzled in for a bit of a cuddle or a stroke, or even better when she has rolled over for a belly rub.

It is then that I strike, and although the exact phrase used varies from occasion to occasion, it goes something like *'oh you must be pregnant, my dog has an uncanny knack as if she can almost smell it, congratulations!'*

I then give them both a wink and leave in complete silence, taking Belle with me, who invariably looks over her shoulder at our hapless victim before giving them a loving but farewell look, which only adds to the effect. Well, what is the point in having a dog if you can't have some fun with her?

Almost on cue, a young lady approached Belle outside of the butcher's shop, and once I had finished my little spiel, her face was a picture.

With time ticking away and feeling the need to put some

miles behind us, it is almost time to move on, though there is just one last thing I wanted to see before we leave. This is the Wensleydale Creamery, well-known of course for making Wensleydale Cheese which is the favourite of perhaps the world's most famous animated dog and his master, Wallace and Gromit.

Although the creamery is certainly a thriving business today, this was not always the case. It almost disappeared completely as far back as the 1930s, and indeed it probably would have had it not been for a man called Kit Calvert, and although not a famous man by any standard, he is quite well-known in Wensleydale.

In 1933, at the height of the great depression, Calvert stepped in after he realized that if the creamery went bankrupt, the local farmers would have nowhere to sell their milk, and as it wasn't cost-effective for each farmer to have their own cheese-making equipment, this would spell disaster for the whole of Wensleydale.

The creamery had, up until then, been owned by a man called Captain Goodwin, an ex-army man, who had bought it on a whim while on holiday here some years earlier. Unfortunately, Goodwin was neither a good cheesemaker nor a successful businessman, and over the years, he gradually found himself in deeper and deeper debt to his suppliers, which were, of course, the local farmers.

This all came to a head in 1933 when a meeting of his creditors was called, who not surprisingly decided to make every possible effort to keep the creamery going so as to ensure continued sales of their milk.

The farmers proved to be somewhat better at running the creamery than Goodwin, and by the end of the year, when the Milk Marketing Board came into being, they had made enough money to clear Goodwin's debts and even had £60 leftover, a princely sum at the time. As part payment for the debts owing to them, each farmer agreed to accept twelve shillings for each pound owed, plus a 16-pound cheese. One old farmer ended up with 76 eight-pound cheeses, far more than he knew what to do with, so he just took the money instead. And perhaps most surprisingly, they gave the business back to Goodwin, along with the £60 profit they had made.

With the Milk Marketing Board now in operation, offering a guaranteed marketplace for the farmers' milk, all initially looked rosy. However, with Goodwin once again proving to be the world's worst businessman, he was soon heavily in debt, this time to the board itself and to the tune of several thousand pounds. The board, perhaps obviously, was not quite as sympathetic as the farmers had been two years earlier, and in 1935 Goodwin saw his business going down the drain, a bit like the milk.

Quite paradoxically, what ultimately saved the creamery was the fact that Goodwin was such a rubbish businessman. For whatever reason, he had somehow managed to stockpile around 150-tons of cheese in the factory, which, even at low prices, was certainly worth at least a small fortune, or so the board thought. However, selling it all at once would cause the price of cheese to plummet.

While the board twiddled their fingers, wondering what to do with possibly the world's largest-ever cheese-mountain, Express Dairies offered to step in, which is where Kit Calvert comes back into the story. He stood up in the marketplace in Hawes and persuaded the farmers not to accept Express Dairies' offer, as it would undoubtedly mean the closure of Hawes Creamery. Kit went further and insisted on collective bargaining on milk prices, as the dairy had been attempting to negotiate with each farmer individually in order to get milk at the lowest possible price. The negotiations dragged on, with both the dairy and Calvert sticking their heels in and with Calvert telling them that the farmers would rather pour their milk down the drain than sell it off to the board at rock-bottom prices.

Calvert ultimately prevailed, and the farmers struck a fair deal, and all that remained was to sort out ownership of the creamery. Express Dairies wanted to dispose of it, so in exchange for paying off the outstanding mortgage, Calvert and the Wensleydale farmers finally managed to get ownership of it, and the only stumbling block had been what to do with the existing cheese mountain still stored throughout the creamery. Quite bizarrely, perhaps, nobody wanted the cheese, and Calvert had to pester the dairy to send a fleet of lorries to remove it, who then swindled a charity in Whitehaven, selling them 20-tons at a knockdown price, but then delivering all 150-tons. It was later said that even the poor and unemployed of the town soon became sick of cheese sandwiches, cheesy mashed potatoes, macaroni and cheese and cheese on toast, among many other recipes that all followed a suspiciously similar theme. If only they knew about pizzas, I found myself thinking.

Calvert took over the running of the business, and although he offered to defer his first year's salary until the company turned a profit, he was surprised when his co-directors initially offered him only one pound a week. At the next board meeting, he asked for three pounds, and his co-directors, in Calvert's own words, nearly threw a fit. While he was reading his newspaper a few days later, he discovered that they had been so angry with him, they had advertised his job.

Not to be outdone, Calvert asserted his right as a director to play his rightful part in selecting his successor, only to fail to turn up for work on the day that the interviews were booked in for. Realizing that they were at something of a stalemate, his co-directors backed down, dismissed the four candidates who had turned up for their interviews and offered Calvert his three-pounds a week. To their absolute horror, however, Calvert refused their belated offering saying he now wanted four pounds a week as well as the job of managing director. They gave in and never challenged his authority again.

Kit Calvert remained the owner of the creamery for many

years. He was well-liked and renowned locally for his practice of giving a job to anyone that wanted one. However, Calvert finally sold out to the Milk Marketing Board in 1966 but continued in control even after this, and although he became a very rich man upon the sale, he insisted on certain safeguards to protect both the creamery and the local economy. One condition that he insisted on was that the creamery would never be closed in his lifetime, and it never did.

However, he died in 1984, after which Dairy Crest took over the running of the creamery. They immediately asset-stripped the place and had closed it completely by 1992, although luckily, it was the subject of a management buy-out six months later, which led to its ultimate success.

When I saw a photograph of Kit Calvert, I could not help but think of the sculpture we had seen on the way into Hawes. In most of his pictures, Calvert can be seen proudly sporting his smoking pipe, which, let's face it, would probably have caused the Hawes busybody to throw another fit.

All was not plain sailing, though, and the creamery was once again soon on the verge of bankruptcy but was miraculously saved when Wallace and Gromit's Oscar-winning movie *A Close Shave* was released in 1995, and indeed, you could say it had a close shave itself. Sales of Wensleydale rocketed, the creamery went from strength to strength, and the rest is history. And apparently, those enterprising monks from back at Askrigg were actually the first to bring this most famous cheese to the dale, though it was originally based on Roquefort cheese and was made with ewe's milk, which of course was often called the *King of Cheese* as well as the *Cheese of Kings*, so there you go.

Wensleydale cheese, in fact nearly all cheeses, nearly vanished completely, however, thanks to the actions of a certain chap called Adolf. While forcing us Brits to eat bland cheese for decades may not have been one of the primary war aims of the Third Reich, it was certainly the outcome of it. At the outset of the Second World War and with the introduction of rationing, the government decided that it would be more efficient and better for everyone if all of the cheesemakers in the country followed the same recipe.

This is how a disgusting abomination called *Government Cheddar* came into being, which was effectively a rubbery, mass-produced, vacuum-packed flavourless lump suitable only for use as a doorstop or as a weapon to hit someone over the head with and was certainly unfit for human consumption. However, you will eat anything when you are hungry, as they say, so it was the only cheese available during the war and for quite some years after. Of course, there was a thriving black market, so if you had the contacts and the means, you could still get hold of some smuggled South American Roquefort, but obviously at a considerable price. Thanks a lot, Adolf.

From there being literally thousands of independent cheesemakers at the outset of the war, there were less than a hundred left when the fighting finally stopped. And even though the war ended in 1945, rationing continued until 1954, by which time many fromagers, for that is the fancy name for cheesemakers, had retired, died or simply forgotten how to make the good stuff. The legacy of this is that we had very few choices available to us right up until the 1990s when as we have heard, a plasticine dog called Gromit helped to fuel something of a renaissance in British cheese, which is something we should all be really grateful for no matter how strange it might sound.

Apparently, there is a visitor centre with lots of Wallace and Gromit themed things to do, but as they don't actually let real dogs in, other than guide dogs, of course, Wensleydale is off the menu for us today. There is lots of other stuff to do here, including art galleries and craft workshops and the like, but we're here to walk, so with that, we are off.

As we left town, Belle was excited by all of the strange smells along the way, and it almost seemed as if she knew that she would be going to lots of new places today, which I guess she did. She was particularly excited when a hedgehog ran across the road in front of us, which surprised me as I thought they would all be hibernating by now, but this one was definitely awake, and it had to be, as cars were coming both ways.

Luckily, it made it to the other side of the road, where it disappeared into a hedge, thereby living up to its name, I guess. Did you know that hedgehogs have not always been called that, by the way? Before they acquired their modern name, they were known as urchins, which explains perfectly why sea urchins are called what they are, don't you think?

Anyway, once it had safely vanished, I popped across the road myself as I wanted to have a quick look at the youth hostel before we left town. A sign in the front garden told passers-by that it had snazzily been renamed *Hostel at Hawes*, which I found just a little pretentious if I am to be truly honest.

I don't mind youth hostels at all, however, and although I would not be staying at any on this trip, they are actually much better places to stay than most people realize, and they are not just for youngsters anymore. Even old fuddy-duddies like me use them. I have stayed in hostels at various places in the Lake District, as well as a rather plush one in Liverpool, and even one in London, although my favourite is definitely the one at Kielder in Northumberland. This one, a re-purposed primary school, is set in the heart of the Kielder Forest Park, an oasis of tranquillity all year round. If you've never stayed in one, you really should try it.

We head out of Hawes to the west, walking a short distance along a somewhat busy road before turning left along a quiet lane that took us up a hill. A stone wall hemmed us in on the right while a small wood on our left allowed Belle the brief opportunity to chase a rabbit that promptly disappeared into a deep, black hole. I could hear an owl high above us somewhere in the trees, and after a minute, I found him and enjoyed watching his head spin around like the exorcist, though without the bad language.

Did you ever wonder why they do that, by the way? Well, it's because they cannot move their eyeballs, and in fact, they don't even have eyeballs but have eyes shaped like tubes, so they are forced to move their heads instead, sometimes up to 270° in either direction, which is quite frankly somewhat freaky when you see it watching you, as this one was me.

We soon found ourselves back in the sheep fields, where we encountered yet another rather rough-looking beast wearing some kind of strap along with a tracking device, though once again, I must admit to being not quite sure exactly what it was. Belle's tail dropped again, though, and she was clearly scared, and I imagine that from the look and the gait of the sheep in question, he was only a step or so away from charging at her, so I am glad she was on her lead.

In the following field, Belle suddenly veered off to my left, and by the time I realized what was going on, it was too late. She had jumped straight into a stream and was already swimming along and biting the water in her usual, customary way.

Alarmingly, the stream passed beneath a dry-stone wall, which Belle was heading straight for, so I called her back, though she promptly ignored me. The water must have suddenly become deeper as she ducked under, and for a moment, my heart stopped as I wondered where she had gone. When her head reappeared a moment later, I knew that she, too, had had enough and was on her way back. At least she would no longer smell like a dead pheasant, I thought.

I quickly ran away from her, and although it was really more of a fast walk that would probably have been quite amusing to anyone watching, I did not care. I just wanted to get out of the way of Belle before she shook several gallons of finest chilled mountain spring water all around, as I had already had a shower before we set off and didn't want another one.

We passed a ramshackle but impressive old barn, which

would have made a good place to stop for lunch had there not been thousands of sheep surrounding it, all eyeing us menacingly for whatever reason, so we carried on, turning north where a sign pointed to Lanacar Lane.

This stretch was a little bit boggy, which was not necessarily a problem, and while I had earlier thought that I had detected the first hint of water in my shoes, I was now sure of it. Don't get me wrong, I had expected to get wet feet at some point, but I just didn't want it to be so early on.

The path weaved through a marsh and down a hill towards the road and valley below, where I could see an old railway bridge, and a village was hidden between the trees beyond that.

Once on Lanacar Lane, which was at the bottom of a small hill, we headed north towards Apersett and soon found the impressive bridge ahead of us.

This was Appersett Viaduct and was definitely worth a quick look. It opened in 1878 but was closed in 1959 and was a continuation of the Wensleydale Railway that we had already walked along between Aysgarth and Hawes.

When it was built, the track forming the Wensleydale Railway was actually owned by two separate companies. The North East Railway owned the line going east out of Hawes, while the Midland Railway owned the line going west. Luckily, they came to a deal that allowed shared use of the track.

There are plans afoot to reopen the railway, with a part of it already fully operational between Northallerton and Redmire at the far eastern end of Wensleydale. Hopefully, sometime soon, you will be able to take a train over this bridge and continue to the west all the way to Garsdale Station, which is the new name for what used to be Hawes Junction, the site of the 1910 disaster, of course. For now, though, we will have to carry on by foot, but I took comfort in the fact that the bridge was in really good condition, so we might well see trains using it again at some point, hopefully in the not-too-distant future.

Appersett itself was a tiny village, and while I looked for a park or at least a bench where we could stop for some lunch, the best I could do was a wall. Unfortunately, it was right next to the road, and as Belle almost tried to jump over it and straight into the traffic, I thought it best to move well away instead.

I fed Belle first, and she wolfed down a full tin of her favourite dog food in no time at all. Hopefully, this would give her the energy she would definitely need this afternoon, as we still had the big climb up Great Shunner Fell to come, which was clearly ahead of us now, rising mightily into the clouds above.

On the tops of the hills around us, there were increasing signs of snowfall, although it was somewhat patchy. Hopefully, this would be no worse at the top, as I really didn't fancy walking through deep snow, and I doubted that Belle did either.

When Belle had finished her own dinner, she eyed up my sandwiches next, watching me closely for any signs of droppage. I saved her the last piece, no more than a tiny morsel, really, but she enjoyed it nonetheless.

We moved on soon enough, as this was just a functional stop to feed ourselves, and there was little to see in Appersett. There had been no one around while we ate, but as I left, I got the impression that we might have had our lunch in someone's back garden after I had noticed some metal poles with washing lines hanging from them. I chuckled to myself as I wondered what I would do if some wandering scruff and his scraggy dog happened across my garden and used it as a picnic site. I'd probably make a brew and go join them, I thought.

Crossing a small stone bridge over Widdale Beck, we initially moved off westwards before turning north almost immediately. Widdale Beck joined the River Ure just a few hundred yards to the north, which we also crossed soon enough before turning off the road completely and onto a footpath that led across vast empty fields and up to Great Shunner Fell. The turn off for the path was at the junction where one road led back to Hardraw less than a mile or so to the east, so in effect, we had almost come in a huge circle. This meant that despite having walked several miles, we were only a mile and a half from where we had been dropped off, which was more than a bit annoying, it has to be said.

While we could have taken the shortcut, the whole point of this walk was to get out and see stuff, and I had really enjoyed walking through Hawes anyway, which would actually be the biggest place we would pass through on this entire walk.

The field was initially flat and very wet. I tip-toed carefully around the very boggy bits while Belle just ploughed fearlessly through, and at the other side, we passed through a small gate and finally began the long climb up to the top of Great Shunner Fell. According to the map, it was around five miles to the summit, but it was hard to tell for sure because of the twisting path.

Belle was back on her lead due to a small herd of sheep, and although I did not know it at the time, these were the last sheep we would see today. They looked sad and forlorn out here in the wilds, but I took comfort that they would sooner or later be somewhere rather warmer, such as in an oven.

The path was barely discernible at this point and more resembled a sheep track, but high up on the hill before me, I could see a gate in the wall, so we headed straight for it, presuming it to be the correct way.

Luckily it was, and it was up on Bluebell Hill that our path met that of the Pennine Way, though there were no bluebells around now. In fact, there was nothing up here, no people, sheep, or even any sound. I had once heard it said that walking was not for everyone, and the evidence for this was more than apparent today in the form of these empty paths that Belle and I had enjoyed exclusive access to, and I am not complaining one bit.

I stopped at the gate to look back at where we had come from and briefly enjoyed the spectacular view down the dale and back to Hawes. The weather was holding off, and although I had felt a few spots of rain on the climb up, it had not yet come to anything, so I crossed my fingers, and we plodded on. The path was becoming much steeper here, and my knees groaned with each step, particularly my right one. If like me, you are advanced in your years, then you may be able to relate to the time when you referred to your knees as left and right, rather than good or bad. Ah, the good old days.

As I have already mentioned, the Pennine Way is one of the longer national trails in the country and is officially recognized as such. However, the section we were currently on was much more than a path and was probably wide enough to drive a tractor on. Who knows, if you're feeling a bit crazy, you might even be able to get two tractors to pass, that is how wide it was, although I am not guaranteeing such antics would not result in not just a nasty accident, but also a couple of angry farmers when they find out that you have been joyriding in their beloved Massey Fergusons.

It would be rude not to think about the Pennine Way for a moment or two, especially while we are stepping on its hallowed ground, and there is quite a lot to learn about it. For instance, did you know that it was Britain's first national trail? Tom Stephenson first mooted the idea in an article in the Daily Herald way back in 1935. In turn, he had been inspired by the Appalachian Way in America that had recently come into existence. He got others involved in the cause, and his efforts ultimately paid off, with the trail being officially opened in April 1965 to much fanfare, with the opening ceremony at one of my favourite places, Malham, being attended by hundreds of people.

Stephenson went on to help form the Ramblers Association, with the idea being to open up the land for everyone rather than to close it off for the elite. We take access for granted nowadays, but it is important to note that this has not always been the case, and one of the most pivotal moments in the campaign was the Kinder Mass Trespass of 1932. This saw hundreds of people from all over the country meet for a walk up Kinder Scout in

Derbyshire, which has now passed into walking folklore. However, some at the time claimed that this kind of action actually hindered the cause. Regardless, the access to land that we enjoy today should not be taken for granted and should instead be cherished and held onto dearly.

The route of the Pennine Way starts in Edale, way down in Derbyshire, and finishes up at Kirk Yetholm in the Scottish Borders. I say up, as you are supposed to walk south to north, and most people spend around two to three weeks leisurely walking the 268 miles or so, with nearly all that finish then enjoying a well-earned pint of beer at The Border Hotel in Kirk Yetholm.

The beer is a tradition initially started by none other than Alfred Wainwright, a famous writer and walker generally remembered for coming up with the original Coast to Coast Walk. He even went so far as to offer to pay for a pint for anyone who managed to walk the full length of the Pennine Way, although at some point his accountant must have had a bit of a breakdown, as this incredible gesture had managed to cost Wainwright tens of thousands of pounds by the time of his death in 1991. Quite surprisingly you can still get a free drink at the hotel when you finish, and although now it is only a half-pint, you do also get a rather nice certificate.

Incredibly, it should be noted that Wainwright wasn't even a fan of the route, famously saying, *You won't come across me anywhere along the Pennine Way*, so perhaps his free pint was just a cunning plan to make people walk it, thereby ensuring that the rest of the countryside remained relatively empty.

I had mentioned that most people take a while to walk this route. Still, just like everything in life, there are some absolute lunatics out there who just want to make us all look bad. These nutters, for that is what they are, have managed to complete the route in a lot less time, and I really do mean a lot less.

For many years, the record holder for the fastest known time was a man called Mike Hartley, who completed the full thing non-stop in a mere 65 hours and 20 minutes or so way back in 1989, which is absolutely astounding when you think about it. Several people tried to beat him over the years, but perhaps not surprisingly, none managed to do so, at least not until well into the following century.

In July 2020, an American named John Kelly finally broke Hartley's record, coming in at 64 hours and 46 minutes, which is again absolutely extraordinary. What is perhaps even more extraordinary is that this record was itself broken by someone else just over a week later. Damian Hall, British author, journalist and general psychopath, finished in 61 hours and 35 minutes. To tell you what kind of a hard man Hall is, it should be noted that he took his newly wedded wife up to Everest Base Camp for their honeymoon. He is a braver man than me, in more ways than one.

However, not to be outdone, Kelly was soon back on the treadmill and training to get his title back, which he did in May of 2021, finishing in just under 58 hours and 5 minutes. Well done to him, I say, but a small part of me keeps wondering whether he just keeps doing it for the free beer at the Border Hotel.

Lastly on this, if 268 miles is not enough, you may be interested in finding out that the Pennine Way now forms a part of a much longer route across Europe. If you have the time and the inclination, you can either carry on north into Scotland and then onto Galway in Ireland, or if you fancy sunnier climes, you can head south to Nice on the Mediterranean coast, which is very nice indeed. Good luck, though, as the whole route is around 3,000 miles long and would take the average walker around six months, unless, of course, your last name is Hartley, Kelly or Hall.

The path led slowly up, and I could see it snake away into the clouds ahead of me and high above. I still wasn't particularly concerned about the weather, as the forecast remained good, bearing in mind it was almost the beginning of winter, and the rain was still holding off, for the time being at least. I had been due to come up here a few days ago but had postponed it due to the weather, and although I was gutted at missing out on the walk last week, it had been the right decision. Not everyone respects the weather, though, and it is actually a fact that hurricanes with female names kill more people than those with male names, purely and simply because people don't respect them as much, seriously.

Belle wandered this way and that, probably still covering two miles for each one I managed, though she still seemed full of energy and was clearly having a good time. Some people moan about applying human characteristics to animals, but it was hard to look at Belle running this way and that and excitedly sniffing puddles, plants and walls without coming to the conclusion that she was happy. Anyway, I don't think happiness is a uniquely human characteristic, and I don't see why other animals, for we are animals too, of course, cannot be happy.

I did feel spots of rain as we slowly trudged on higher and higher, but they came to nothing, and I did not need to break out the waterproofs. I did, however, notice a drop in temperature as we got higher, so I just wrapped my scarf around my neck, which made me feel immediately warm again.

We came across a fingerpost pointing down and to the left, which directed walkers to Cotterdale, at which point a quick glance at my map allowed me to know my exact location, and we continued on and up towards the right.

It dawned on me that we had not seen anyone for a while, and for a moment, I wondered if everyone else knew something I didn't, though I soon dismissed this thought and reasoned instead that everyone else had decided to simply stay at home on what was not exactly a great day for walking.

Don't get me wrong, the weather wasn't that bad, although it was gloomy and dark, but regardless of this, I only had today available to come here and no other day, so if I wished to do this walk, it had to be today.

Other commitments beckoned, including such rude interruptions to my life as work, and what with Christmas just around the corner, it was now or never.

The main problem, however, was transport. I have already explained that Belle is not the world's best driver, so I instead had to blag a lift from someone else. That someone else was my dear old dad, accompanied by my mum, who had both joined me in the car for the journey to Sedbusk. After dropping me off, they would go and do some sightseeing for the day in Hawes and Hardraw and wherever else, and then meet Belle and myself at either Keld or Thwaite at the end of the day.

This solved the problem of me parking the car in Hawes and somehow having to find my way back to it at the end of the walk, which had proven to be very difficult, to say the least. Public transport from Keld to Hawes did not really exist, and after enquiring about a taxi which I was told would cost rather more than I was willing to pay, I had decided instead to keep the money and buy a rather large bar of gold or perhaps half of Yorkshire instead. The solution, then, was to offer my parents a free day out in exchange for a quick pick-up at the end of the day.

I had told them that I would know where I would finish by mid-afternoon and would let them know accordingly, and while I hoped to get to Keld, at the back of my mind was the fact that we had added the extra miles from Sedbusk onto this morning's walk, and I was concerned that this would then mean we would not get as far as we had hoped. I say we, but I don't think Belle would care how far we would get until she became tired, of course, when she would simply want to stop regardless of where she happened to be.

I think this was when I first realized that we would not get to Keld, although I still hoped we would, and I was perhaps in denial of how far we still had to go. I had seen a fingerpost sign that said it was just over six miles to the top of Great Shunner

Fell, more than I had thought, which considering the mileage required to get to Thwaite, put Keld more or less out of reach, at least for today, and was further than I had thought we had left to go. On the map, the top of the fell was around two-thirds of the way from Hawes to Thwaite, although I noticed that it was barely halfway to Keld.

We plodded on further and further, slowly getting higher, which also meant one other thing – the views simply got better too. Hills, dales and valleys were all around, and visibility was still pretty good despite the misty conditions.

As we walked through the miles, sometimes with Belle leading the way and sometimes with me in front, the path alternated several times between muddy track and flagstone path. Every now and then, all traces of any path seemed to disappear completely, and we simply found ourselves tramping through the heather that dominated these upland fells.

At these points, where there was no obvious path to follow, people seemed to have used various routes to get to the next bit of proper path, and this certainly appeared to be damaging the flora of the area. Interestingly, the higher we got, the wetter the ground became, especially where there was no defined path, and while I hopped from one clump of soil to the next, Belle splashed and sploshed straight through without a care in the world. How she didn't feel the cold, I have no idea.

One particular stretch of flagstone path proved very interesting indeed, as we more or less found ourselves walking up a river, or more accurately, a series of waterfalls. I christened it Little Niagara, and while Belle just carried on regardless, I made a series of futile attempts to jump across the fast-flowing water, and where this was impossible, I tried to wade through the shallowest bits.

I was still wearing my ever so comfortable and trusty Merrell walking shoes, which was perhaps not the best idea, as I had managed to rip a couple of holes in them while tackling the West

Highland Way a few months back. They were, however, very comfortable and had only recently become worn in, so I reckoned that I could get away with wearing them for a day walk, so long as that walk was somewhat dry. This walk, however, was rapidly becoming anything but dry, and my feet seemed to be completely sodden by now.

Patches of snow became more and more common as we made our way to the top of the fell, and eventually, we began to encounter it along the path itself. I was not sure what Belle would make of it, as she had not really seen much of the stuff and certainly had never walked considerable distances through it, though I remembered that she did enjoy eating snowballs a couple of winters ago.

The first patch of snow we came across, therefore, became a laboratory, or perhaps a labradoratory, to be more exact. I encouraged Belle onto what was a rather large patch of the frozen white stuff, and as she tentatively stepped forwards, I could tell that she was not entirely sure.

She sniffed the surface below her and tried once or twice to take a bite. As she arced around to return to me, she encountered a bit that was clearly not quite as frozen as the rest. Her front paws broke the surface and disappeared into what was apparently quite a deep snowdrift. Her head followed, and she looked a bit shocked as she scrambled around trying to drag herself out, all while she was listening to a chubby old bloke laugh behind her, which was, of course, me. I know I may be a little cruel by saying this, but sometimes Belle is about as useful as a white crayon.

We carried on upwards, with a firm mist now moving in all around us, and I briefly wondered whether or not I should put Belle on a lead, but decided not to as she seemed to be keeping such a close distance to me, to the point where I almost considered changing her name to shadow.

The snow became more widespread, and drifts crossing the

path were more frequent, and at one steep stretch shortly before the summit, I almost considered turning back. I usually walk with a couple of trekking poles, nothing fancy, but useful anyway when out in the wilds, such as we were now. This is also where I wished I had bought one of those homemade walking sticks back near Hardraw, as I slipped and slid while I attempted to make my way up.

The drift was clearly quite deep, and much of the surface had frozen, forming a crust of ice that was thick in places but not so in others. Treading very carefully, I was doing really well until I was mid-way across, when the ice gave way beneath my feet, and I fell forwards, causing me to lurch down towards the ground, considerably assisted by both gravity and some extra kilos I had acquired last Christmas and had not managed to get rid of just yet. My head followed, and I felt a bit shocked as I scrambled around trying to drag myself out, and all the while, I could hear a chubby old dog laughing behind me, which was, of course, Belle.

Finally, back on the path, and after frantically looking around to ensure there were no witnesses to my feebleness that would need to be eliminated before they told everyone of my utter incompetence up here, possibly by tossing them over the side of the mountain, I regained my composure and decided that if we came across another obstacle such as that, we were turning back.

Luckily, the path from here was good, and it soon flattened out into a plateau, and in the distance, I could finally see the shelter that marked the summit of Great Shunner Fell. I told Belle we had made it, though she totally failed to get excited, so we plodded on the last few hundred yards and stopped at the shelter to finish the lunch we had started at Appersett.

I had a couple of sandwiches left, whereas Belle had eaten all of her slop back down there, but that was her problem, I thought, as I stuffed ham, cheese and pickle into my cake-hole.

Unfortunately, those big, round doggy-eyes soon got the better of me, and in no time at all, she had somehow fleeced me of yet more of my lunch, including half of my sausage roll.

Luckily, she did not like Kendal Mint Cake, so I enjoyed this myself, hoping it would give me the energy needed to get back down to the other side. It's amazing stuff, and it had possibly saved my life on the last day of our recent walk along the West Highland Way, when I had foolishly set off without breakfast, under the patently false impression that I was superhuman and did not need to worry about such frivolities. The cake kept me going until my good friend Robin saw how pale I was, after which he somehow cooked up a chilli con carne in the middle of one of the most remote Scottish glens imaginable, which finished the job of bringing me back to life.

Anyway, the shelter wasn't a building as such but was just a series of three walls forming a sort of cross shape, which was actually quite effective at keeping the wind at bay, assuming you moved to the appropriate leeward side. There were benches, too, but they were obviously very wet, and as I did not want a soggy behind for the next few miles, I simply stood while Belle ate the last of my lunch. My mind drifted off to stories I had read and heard about this mighty mountain, which I will share with you now, and which I promise will be worth it.

Great Shunner Fell is the third highest mountain in the Yorkshire Dales after Whernside and Ingleborough, and it should therefore not be underestimated. At over 2,300 feet high, the weather at the top can change at the drop of a hat, so if you don't have a hat, you might find yourself in a spot of bother. Mine was somewhere in my backpack, but I certainly didn't need it today.

The fell is eight miles long, and the Pennine Way traverses almost all of it, which was, of course, the path we followed up here and which we will follow down the other side to Thwaite. This will also be the highest point on the Herriot Way, so if you ever come up here when it is a bit clearer than today, the views will allow you to see as far as Cumbria to the west and County Durham to the east.

Although it doesn't look like a mountain as such, it really is one, which reminds me of another mountainous link to this area. As we had passed through Hawes, I had seen a road sign for Burtersett, which is just a mile or so to the east of the town.

Although it is a tiny, nondescript sort of place, Burtersett is the historical home of the Hillary family, and although most of them were stuffy old rich people, a couple are certainly worthy of mention. William Hillary is the first one, who became quite well known in the world of tropical diseases. If you remember, we briefly encountered him earlier, and while we thought we had heard the last of the doctors of Wensleydale, he is the last one, I promise you.

He started his career in Ripon, which I have to say was not particularly tropical the last time I passed through, but with global warming, you never know what's coming. Eventually, he ended up out in Barbados, which is certainly a touch more tropical than Ripon surely, and spent his time there studying tropical sprue. If you don't know what that is, then take a deep breath because I am ever so sorry to have to tell you that he spent his time playing around with diarrhoea, so he sort of paved the way for the work of those that followed him, including, of course, Sir Christopher Booth, who followed in his somewhat messy footsteps. I know that Diarrhoea is not necessarily the nicest of subjects and that sometimes you're better off not knowing, but anyway, you're welcome.

While in Barbados, he was also the personal physician to George Washington, who went on to become the first president of the United States, making him yet another dales doctor who, no matter how unlikely this may seem, had somehow managed to befriend one of the most powerful men in the history of that fine country. We can also assume that he probably spent at least some of his time playing with the Perkin's Tractor that the President had recently wasted five guineas on, but nobody's perfect, as they say.

But what has that got to do with mountains, I hear you ask. Well, not a lot, but there is a further link with the Hillary family and mountains, which is, of course, Sir Edmund Hillary, the first person ever to have managed to scramble all the way to the top of Mount Everest, the highest mountain in the world, although not on his honeymoon, it should be noted. His grandparents came from Yorkshire, and more specifically from Burtersett, until they emigrated to New Zealand, never to look back.

Back to Great Shunner Fell, however, and someone had told me to look out for small pieces of coal at the summit as it was mined in several places up here until the 1880s. This end date coincided with the opening of the Wensleydale Railway, of course, and this made it much easier to get hold of better-quality coal which was also cheaper, from elsewhere in the country.

Although I didn't see any coal, the view from the top was amazing as the clouds briefly parted. Mountains were all around, including in the east Wild Boar Fell, which is supposedly where the last ever wolf in England was killed, although this is far from certain. You think they would have called it Wild Wolf Fell if it really had been here. It gets its name from the fact that a wild boar was certainly caught there, and if you don't believe me, pop along to the church in Kirkby Stephen to see its tusk. I certainly couldn't see Cumbria or County Durham from up here today, however.

What I could see, though, just to the northeast and barely visible through the misty clouds, was Hugh Seat, the tenth-highest mountain in Yorkshire, apparently. I had come across this mountain during the summer that had just left us, when Rob and myself had ventured up the backbone of England in an electric car, trying to trace the course of the watershed, and Hugh Seat is significant in this regard. On its slopes are the sources of two major rivers, with the first being the Eden that heads northwest and joins the River Esk at Carlisle before emptying out into the Solway Firth and then the Irish Sea. The second is the River Swale, which both gives its name to and then flows through Swaledale before joining the Rivers Ure and Ouse. Finally, it empties into the North Sea via the Humber Estuary, which is, of course, my own stomping ground.

It was thought that the River Ure also has its source up on Hugh Seat, but this is actually on the neighbouring hill of Ure Head, which is perhaps not surprising given the name. Anyway, it is not surprising that this mountain has been nicknamed the *Watershed of England*, but there is much more to the mountain than that, and it is to do with its name.

The mountain, you see, was named after Hugh de Morville, and while you may not have heard of him as such, he became pretty notorious in the 12th century during the reign of King Henry II when he, along with three co-conspirators, murdered Thomas Beckett, the Archbishop of Canterbury.

Apparently, they misinterpreted the king's comments when he casually asked one day, '*will no one rid me of this turbulent priest?*' Other accounts say what he actually said was, '*what miserable drones and traitors have I nourished and brought up in my household, who let their lord be treated with such shameful contempt by a low-born cleric?*'

Either way, what Hugh de Morville heard instead was, '*please go and chop the archbishop up, thank you very much.*'

So it was off to Canterbury that de Morville went, along with three other knights, and together they confronted Beckett in the cathedral, ordering him to go to Winchester to account for himself before the king. Beckett refused to go, however, so as perhaps a kind of persuasion technique, one of the knights chopped the top of Beckett's head off, or as they put it, *sliced off the summit of his crown*. When Beckett still refused to move, they removed more or less all of the top of his head, apparently *turning his blood white with his brains and his brains white with his blood*. After this, and as if it wasn't enough, a cleric who had accompanied the knights then put his foot on Beckett's neck to hold him firm and proceeded to spread Beckett's brains all around the church, after which he said probably one of the most unnecessary phrases that has ever been muttered at the site of a murder, and which was *we can leave this place, knights, he will not get up again.* No shit, Sherlock.

With the dastardly deed done, the king basically told de Morville that it would probably be best if he vanished, so he went off to Rome to seek forgiveness from the Pope. However, perhaps not surprisingly, this forgiveness wasn't exactly forthcoming, and the Pope instead told de Morville and the other knights to go to Jerusalem barefoot and thereafter live alone in the hills. I'll be honest with you, this doesn't sound like a whole lot of fun, and I suspect that Hugh probably thought that the king was being more than a little bit ungrateful, but at least he has a boggy hill named after him in Yorkshire.

Anyway, back to the walk, and the popularity of the Pennine Way, which of course currently merges with the Herriot Way at this point, has actually done considerable ecological damage to the fell, as I had already hinted at on our walk up here, and this has reportedly led to a strip of land 200 feet wide being eroded away by the thousands of people who come up here every year, myself included. Thankfully, work to address this problem has now begun, and the flagstone paths have given at least some of the surrounding moorland the chance to finally begin its recovery.

While we are up here, it seemed only right to mention a plane that crashed hereabouts way back in January 1943. It was at the height of the Second World War that a Halifax bomber took off from RAF Leeming, approximately 30-miles east of here, on a cross-country training exercise. Onboard were seven men who were a mixture of British and Canadian personnel.

All went well until the aircraft attempted to return to base, but the pilot found the airfield and the surrounding area completely shrouded in cloud. Not knowing their exact location, they somehow managed to end up further west than they thought they were, which became a huge problem when the crew decided to drop below the cloud in an attempt to discover their true location.

The aircraft hit the slopes of Great Shunner Fell somewhere above Thwaite, and immediately burst into flames. Of the seven crew on board, three were killed instantly, and only one managed to escape from the wreckage. This was Air Gunner Clinton Pudney, who, because of what followed, became a true hero.

Pudney possibly survived because he was assigned as the mid-gunner that day. As the title implied, he was manning the gun in the middle of the aircraft, which stuck above the fuselage in a little bubble.

Although badly injured, having suffered severe lacerations to his face with considerable blood loss, and as well as being in shock, Pudney nonetheless re-entered the burning wreckage and somehow managed to pull out all six of his colleagues. Although, as has already been said, three were dead, Pudney managed to rescue the pilot Edmond LeFebvre, the flight engineer Hugh McGeach, and his fellow air gunner John Askew.

That is not the end of it, though. Once they were at a safe distance from what was left of the aircraft, Pudney then set off over open moorland. We should remember this was in the middle of January, and despite being injured, he walked around two miles in order to raise the alarm.

The survivors were taken to the hospital at nearby Catterick Garrison, where Askew sadly died of his injuries a short while later, though the others managed to recover from theirs.

For his valour, Pudney was awarded the George Medal, the second-highest award for bravery in non-combat situations. All three went on to fight for their country once more; however, spoiler warning, things didn't end all that well.

In a rather sad and perhaps quite bizarre twist of fate, Pudney was involved in a very similar crash less than six months later. Finding himself in another Halifax, this aircraft was struck by lightning and crashed at Clenchwarton near King's Lynn in Norfolk. Once again, Pudney managed to pull his mates from the wreckage of the bomber and again walked off to find help. Sadly, he had less luck this time, and he died from his injuries along with all of his fellow crew members. He was only 21 years old.

Hugh McGeach was also soon back in the air again, this time with 428 *Ghost* Squadron, but in July 1943, he boarded his last flight. Yet another Halifax, this one was shot down over enemy territory, and along with his crew, McGeach ended up as a prisoner of war. Unfortunately, despite extensive searches, it is not clear what happened to Hugh after he was taken prisoner, although he did end up in Stalag Luft 6, a prisoner of war camp on the coast of the Baltic Sea in what is now Lithuania. Life in there was certainly not easy, and the winters were long and cold, but the reports I have read about the place state that the men were treated pretty well, all in all.

And in an attempt to end on a positive note regarding this little story, we come finally to the pilot, Edmond LeFebvre. Once Pudney had helped him out of the wreckage, LeFebvre assisted him in getting the others out, but could not manage the walk to Thwaite due to his injuries, so he stayed and cared for McGeach and Askew as best as he could.

Once recovered from his injuries, LeFebvre went on to serve with 424 Squadron and was awarded the Distinguished Flying Cross in 1945 for devotion to duty, skill, and fortitude. At the end of the war, he went home to Canada, lived a long and happy life, and died just after his 80th birthday in 2000.

There, I told you it was worth it.

Anyway, we had been up here long enough, and it was time to move on. I was already beginning to feel the chill from standing still, so in what seemed no time at all, we were once again on our way, although this time heading down the mountain.

This was when I decided that we would definitely not make it to Keld. The mileage we still had left suggested that we would get to Thwaite just as it was beginning to get dark. The stretch of footpath from Thwaite to Keld involved yet another three miles or so of walking, including a rather big climb over the bulk of Kisdon Hill, although it did not actually go all the way to the summit, but would nonetheless be too far for us to do today.

Therefore, while I was on high ground and still had a scrap of phone signal left, I sent a text asking for a pick-up in Thwaite, and prayed that it would go through at some point.

The long walk down started shallow but soon became very steep. The path, much of which was paved with flagstones, was a help, although once again, it soon became a stream of fast-moving water. I had, by now, realized that my feet were pretty soggy, so I had given up any and all hopes of keeping them dry, and as I figured we were on the last leg of this walk, I splashed along with a complete lack of caution through puddles and streams, much the same as what Belle had been doing all day long.

After maybe a mile or two, I noticed a lush and fertile looking valley down to my right, which meant it was to my east. I figured this was where we were heading, though it looked so far away at the moment. Still, I sought solace in that the end was at least in sight.

Somewhere slightly below us and to the right of this valley is Buttertubs Pass, a high mountain pass linking Hawes with Keld and Muker. The Buttertubs part of the name comes from some rather deep pot-holes high up on the pass, and allegedly get their name from years ago when farmers taking butter to the market would stop here and hang their butter in the pot-holes in order to cool it, which sounds to me to be both a lot of hard work and highly impractical, but you never know. In between, the road twists and turns and rises and falls for around 5-miles and is a great place to bring the kids and try to make them throw up in the back of the car.

Anyway, it has become sort of famous in recent years for various reasons. 1970s folk singer Mr Fox sang about Buttertubs Pass in his song *The Gipsy*, which tells the heavy tale of a young man desperately trying to track down a beautiful gipsy girl who has stolen his heart. He chases her through these hills, and as I listened to the song, I plotted their route on a map, and he does indeed chase the love of his life through this very pass, although, quite sadly, ultimately to no avail.

The pass has become even more famous in recent years, too. None other than Jeremy Clarkson has ripped up the tarmac in various cars on more than one occasion before his untimely exit from Top Gear, of course. In fact, he declared it *England's only spectacular road*, so there you go. One of the best places to view it from is the seat just where the road takes you from Wensleydale into Swaledale and the valley below, and from here, you can watch cars, vans and cyclists crashing off the road and disappearing into the ditches all day long. I wondered if this is where Clarkson had been on that fateful day that ended not so well at Simonstone Hall, and I imagine it probably was.

The Tour de France has also passed this way, presumably almost as fast as Jeremy Clarkson. It amazes me how these lycra-clad lunatics manage to go so fast, and I have heard bizarre but true stories of speed limits being relaxed in order to not criminalise these crazy clowns. Another famous race was supposed to be held here, too. The UCI 2019 World Championships, which is basically the world championships for bicycle road racing, should have passed through Buttertubs Pass as more or less a blur, but it had to be cancelled because it was raining. This is really surprising, and by that, I mean not the fact that it was raining, as it rains up here all the time, but the fact that they had cancelled it because of that reason. I guess they just never thought it through beforehand.

As the path slowly turned to the right, and as we passed a

couple of piles of stones which were shown on my map, I was able to figure out that we had around three miles still to go, which meant we would definitely walk into Thwaite just as it was getting dark.

Halfway down the hill, when I checked my phone, I was horrified to see that my message had not gone through, and worse still, I had no signal whatsoever. I re-sent it hoping that it would somehow get there, and as I walked along, I wondered whether my lift would be pointlessly waiting for me in Keld instead. This would not be an ideal outcome, I thought to myself, as I splashed along in my now waterlogged shoes, my feet squelching with every step.

We passed a small waterfall, which Belle tried to jump into, but I called her back, and she surprisingly obeyed. She had probably more or less dried out from her previous soaking, and assuming we would be getting into the car within the next hour, I did not want her getting any wetter.

The path widened as we dropped down into the valley below, and in the distance, I could see that some cars were already using their headlights and that some of the houses in the village were also now illuminated.

The last mile seemed the longest, as it usually does, so it was a grateful feeling indeed when we finally hit tarmac and saw roof tiles through the trees down in the village below us.

We had only half a mile or so to go, and with Belle back on her lead due to the road, I was surprised when she suddenly shot off ahead of me, almost dragging me along with her. When I looked up, I was surprised to see our two intrepid taxi drivers, and I knew then that within just a few minutes, I would be sitting in a nice warm car with the heater on, and it would be pointing at my feet, that is for sure. Before we left, though, I noticed the Kearton Hotel, which reminded me that the Kearton name has strong links with the village, and which meant we had one last story to tell for the day.

Thwaite, you see, was the home of two people you have probably never heard of but perhaps really should have. The rather boringly named Richard Kearton and his much more imaginatively named brother Cherry were born here way back in the late 1800s and became rather famous in their day, and were ultimately one of the inspirations for none other than David Attenborough. They were both incredibly fascinated with the wildlife that surrounded them and happened to be also very interested in the emerging technology of photography, and they rather cannily decided to merge the two.

In the process, they became the first people to photograph many types of animals, both wild and domestic, and wrote many illustrated books on the subject, which became rather popular and, quite handily, earned them a pound or two in the process. They also dabbled in audio recordings using a primitive phonograph, which is basically a very old record player, so they also enjoy the distinction of having recorded the earliest known sounds of birds singing in the wild in 1900.

They had a good system of working together, with Cherry taking most of the pictures and Richard writing the actual books, but their interest also went wider than just animals. For instance, Cherry recorded the first film of London from the air, and when the First World War broke out, he hopped straight over to Antwerp with his camera and recorded the first combat footage of the war. Much of this was done with homemade equipment and a fair bit of improvisation, such as tripods made from bamboo or with Cherry simply sitting on Richard's shoulders in order to get a shot.

What they are really remembered for, however, is their innovative design of hides which were made from actual animals such as sheep and ox. They had the animals killed and prepared by a taxidermist and then spent many long hours hiding inside them with a camera while waiting for other inquisitive creatures to come and have a sniff, which was both successful and highly entertaining, I imagine. I do wonder which hole they stuck the camera out of, though, but perhaps that is just me? Later on, apparently, they used other disguises, including a tree and even a rubbish dump, which, let's face it, are not bad ideas.

However, one of the Kearton brothers' biggest jobs was accompanying none other than the 26th President of the United States on a safari adventure across much of East Africa in 1910. Landing in Mombasa, they spent months with Theodore Roosevelt tracking and shooting big-game across much of what is now Kenya and Uganda. The Keartons managed to get some amazing footage of all of this, as well as clips of encounters with the local Maasai people, though they did incorrectly call them Zulus at the time because this sounded much more exciting.

The Smithsonian-Roosevelt African Expedition then was incredibly big news at the time, and lots of people tried to cash in on the popularity of it, even to the extent of a rival American film company releasing a fake documentary purporting to be the real expedition, but which had actually been filmed in a wildlife park in California using a lookalike actor as a stand-in for the former president. Still, nobody was fooled, at least not for long, and the subsequent real documentary released by Pathe Films offers a truly amazing window into the president's life. Of course, much of it was filmed by Cherry Kearton, who was born right here in Thwaite.

Finally, as has already been hinted at, none other than much-loved naturalist Sir David Attenborough had previously spoken highly of the Kearton brothers. He had even gone so far as to say he was directly inspired by their pioneering work and inventive means way before anyone else had thought of doing such things with cameras and animals. I'm not sure what his thoughts would be, however, on the idea of shooting an elephant, scooping out its innards and hiding in it to take pictures of lions, although I suspect they would not necessarily be positive ones.

We were indeed back at the car in just a few more minutes, and Belle jumped in first and took her usual place on the back seat. Luckily, the smell of dead pheasant did not accompany us on the journey home, although the smell of wet dog was bad enough, quite frankly.

All in all, we had had another good day and had once again been very lucky with the weather. The mileage setback from last time had clearly carried over to today, and this is something we would definitely have to address on the next stage of our walk, which would be from Thwaite to Reeth via Keld. Of course, at some point before that, we would have to decide which route we would take, as there is a high route and a low route, though that is definitely a question for another day.

Lastly, as we set off on the long drive home, we stopped ever so briefly at Buttertub's Pass, which we had mentioned earlier, of course. The road from Thwaite back to Hawes is not for the faint-hearted, especially when driving north to south, as the drop down to the valley below is both impressive and terrifying at the same time, with a rather insubstantial piece of wire and the occasional post being the only thing that separates you and your car from certain death along this steep and winding road.

After seeing this road firsthand, I'm guessing that Jeremy Clarkson probably was filming here at the time of his stay at Simonstone Hall, as it is one of the most impressive roads in the country, and Buttertub's itself is also worth a look. A waterfall cascades into a seemingly bottomless hole in the ground, and indeed, Victorian guides once regaled visiting tourists with claims that *some of the Buttertubs were bottomless, and some were deeper than that.* As I mentioned this fact, Belle was already asleep and snoring loudly on the back seat of the car, and she didn't wake up until we pulled up at home almost three hours later.

HIGH OR LOW

Thwaite to Reeth: The Low Route

I picked Rob up at some ridiculous hour, and by the time the dawn light finally started to break around us, we were well into North Yorkshire following a rather long and thankfully uneventful drive.

Snow-capped hills and mountains beckoned us in the distance, which was a pleasant surprise we had not expected, as none had been forecast but was welcome nonetheless. I drove much the same route as for the first two legs of this walk but turned north at Leyburn instead of west, today heading for Reeth.

We nearly didn't get there, as halfway across Redmire Moor, the road turned into an ice-rink, forcing us to divert back up to Richmond. At one point, my car was slipping backwards down an icy hill, though thankfully no one was stupid enough to have followed us in our folly, and although my brakes failed to stop the car, I did manage to at least keep it on the road, but only just. It was at this point that I remembered, admittedly a tad too late perhaps, how Herriot had described the roads of Yorkshire as often impassable in the winter. I guess I should have listened.

Reeth was surprisingly busy for such an early hour on what was probably the coldest day of the year so far. I can say that with confidence, as we were in the first week of January, and standing on the village green, which was of course now white, and looking at the snow on the mountains all around us, was definitely something of a treat, with the white of the peaks contrasting with the deep blue sky that hung above us.

The plan was to get the little white bus once again, this time to Thwaite, where Belle and myself had finished just a few days before, although, as I have already mentioned, my good friend Rob would be joining us for the rest of the journey. He had wanted to do the full walk with me, but other commitments had meant this had been impossible, and I think he was at least a little surprised that I had not managed to get lost and die in the wilderness without his navigational skills. He had complained vigorously that I had not invited him on the last leg, though I had presumed him to be at work that day, but anyway, he was here now, and we could therefore get lost and die in the frozen wilderness together. Anyway, from Thwaite, we would head up and over Kisdon Hill to Keld, where a right turn would take us over the tops of yet more hills and mountains back down to Reeth, via Gunnerside Moor and Melbecks Moor. It was quite simple, and all we had to do was keep putting one foot in front of the other. What could possibly go wrong?

After quickly checking in the village shop as to the location of the bus stop, which was apparently and quite luckily directly outside of the shop, I suggested to Rob that we hang about out- side while we waited for the bus in order to acclimatise to the cold conditions.

Belle, however, had something to say about this. She had been happily asleep on the back seat of the car all of the way here, only stirring from her deep slumber for just a few seconds when she was probably wondering why the hell the car was going back- wards down a hill at quite some speed. Anyway, as I opened the door for her to get out, she just sat there and refused to budge. Even after calling her name, she still remained indignant and simply tucked her paws and tail even further beneath her body before putting her head back down and pretending to go back to sleep.

Rob and I had no choice, then, but to get back into the car and wait inside, which was actually still quite warm and therefore not a bad idea at all, Belle, thank you very much. I had hoped there might be a small café to wait in, but could not see one, as on the way here I had suggested to Rob that we start the day with a nice hot chocolate. There was a tea-room in Thwaite, though, so we would no doubt get one there, as it would be a little later in the day, and everything would surely be open by then.

We remained inside until a minute or two before the bus was due, at which point we went back outside into the icy sunshine, coaxing Belle out with a small biscuit, and which was, funnily enough, the exact moment that the bus pulled up, which I took as a good omen. It actually stopped right behind our car too, which I also took as a sign.

Asking the driver if he was going to Thwaite, he assured us that he would try his best, and I am not sure if he was joking, given the treacherous conditions that we had already encountered on our own particular journey earlier that morning.

We sat at the back of the small bus and were soon joined by an older couple who also looked set for a day's walking and who Belle spent the next half-hour or so trying to creep towards.

The journey to Reeth was interesting, though I kept finding myself wondering if this little bus of ours would actually make it. There were countless things that could go wrong. We could skid to our death on a patch of ice, or perhaps an oncoming car would plough into us from beyond a sharp and fatal bend. Maybe we would just bounce off the road completely on one of the many sharp hills, and perhaps, if we were really lucky, it would be a combination of all of the above.

Somehow still in one piece, the bus pulled to a halt, and as Rob and myself wondered if this was our stop and as Belle stood up, clearly eager to get off, the driver told us that we were in fact at Gunnerside, and we would have to wait here for a minute or so as we had arrived slightly ahead of schedule. Looking around, there was absolutely nobody around, but we waited nonetheless.

Sure enough, just a minute later, we moved off once again, soon blasting straight through Muker before finally hitting Thwaite a short while later.

I recognized the village from my last visit, and as I looked around the bus for a button to press to signal to the driver to stop, I momentarily panicked when I could not find one, and not being a regular user of buses, I had no idea what to do under such circumstances. Thinking on my feet, and I am quite proud of this, I instead opted to shout *ding ding*, much to the amusement of Rob and my fellow passengers. The silliness had started, I thought to myself.

Belle once again launched herself off the bus, skidding on the frozen path outside. I enjoyed a little chuckle before I too went for a little slide, only to regain my footing a split second later, thereby avoiding an early morning embarrassment. I considered giving Rob the warning about the slippery path, but as he was still messing around at the back of the bus, he probably wouldn't have heard me anyway, so I didn't bother.

As he carefully stepped down from the bus then, I had my camera in hand, ready for the inevitable skid, and even better, he had his hands full with his backpack and hiking poles as well as his phone. This was going to be fun, I thought, as his foot impacted the shiniest piece of black ice possible, and as he let go of the hand-rail . . . nothing.

The automatic door of the bus hissed to a close, the driver pulled away, and we were left alone in Thwaite, which was silent at this time of the day. Hiding my disappointment that Rob had not fallen face-first to the floor, I mentioned to him that we were out of luck with the tea room, which was across the road and quite visibly closed, and that we would have to wait a while longer for our hot chocolate, which we would maybe get at Keld, where we could probably warm up in the pub, Keld Lodge.

Before we headed off, I put Belle's coat onto her, which she did not seem too keen on, but which she was definitely going to need today. She is not normally a fan of such things, but even I felt the cold under my many layers, so I could only imagine what she must be feeling, being completely naked, if you know what I mean. I'm sure dogs don't feel the cold like we do, and I had even read that they have a cunning system that prevents their feet from getting cold, which is a bit like a mini central heating system. Small blood veins called venules run alongside the main arteries and act as a heat exchanger, thereby maintaining the temperature of the main blood vessels flowing through a dog's feet, thus ensuring that they don't feel the cold as much as we do. Simples. Humans, on the other hand, have no such comforts, which is why we wear shoes, I guess. I'm not sure how long I would last out here without footwear, but I'm guessing not long.

Moving on, the path led to the east, out of the village, and we were soon in and out of small fields and immediately passing through the tiny gates and squeezes that seemed to dominate this landscape, and which by now we were so familiar with.

I was glad to see that Rob was finding getting through each of these small gates even more of a challenge than what it was for me, so I obviously let him go first in order to observe the fun. Belle remembered them from last time, evidently, though she seemed to be lacking her manners today, regularly pushing in front of Rob as soon as he opened any given gate.

We were soon heading straight up the hill as well, which was good in that the effort would warm us up, but bad in that it might well finish us off.

The hill in question was Kisdon Hill, though it is definitely a mountain, and the plan was to follow it up and around in a clockwise manner before heading down into Keld at the other side in search of that elusive hot chocolate. This seemed straightforward enough, and as we got higher, the views soon became quite spectacular, though this time, each scene was complete with a winter dusting of snow.

I had noticed on the map an interesting sounding feature

called the *Dungeon,* which we were passing by now. While I had been quite childishly looking forward to discovering the basement of a secret castle or some other interesting feature that I could tell my grandchildren about in years to come, the reality was unfortunately far less interesting. It turns out that the dungeon in question is actually just an old barn, and as barns were often named after the field in which they stood, the dungeon on the map also signifies the name of this field. By the way, on a slightly different note, I feel compelled to say that I don't have any grandchildren, and due to the experiences I went through with my own kids, I don't particularly want that chapter in my life to come any time soon, thank you very much.

Soon enough, the snow began to get quite deep, at least in places, and I wondered what Belle would make of it. However, when I turned to see where she was, she was clearly having fun, darting this way and that in a manner that seemed somewhat random and bore little resemblance to our path.

Once again doing three steps for each one that we took, she was clearly having lots and lots of fun, biting and eating the snow as she went, and was absolutely in her element.

Rob and I, on the other hand, were not. This rude awakening, up a very steep hill, was making us huff and puff in a manner somewhat reminiscent of the big bad wolf having an asthma attack, and the going was made even harder by the fact that we were walking through snow, of course. Now I'm not sure if walking through snow is harder than walking through soft sand along a beach, but when you add in the fact that we were also heading straight up a steep hill, it became a no brainer. This was much harder indeed.

The path twisted this way and that, as did Belle, though Rob and myself tried to make as straight a line as possible across each field so as not to add any unnecessary steps onto our journey. As we went into each field, we would look for the gate at the other side and head straight for it, while Belle constantly chose the scenic route.

There were no sheep around today, they had probably all been moved lower down in the dale or stowed safely away in barns, so Belle had free rein in each field, something that she was clearly enjoying. The hills didn't seem to bother her either, but once again, it should be remembered that she had four-wheel drive, and I was quite jealous as I watched her move effortlessly ahead of us.

Passing a small wood and then a farm, the path became even steeper as we took a left turn up a small lane lined either side with dry-stone walls. This served to make the route fairly clear, at least for now, but when we came to a gate, I suggested to Rob that we should go through it, which was a complete mistake. Ten minutes later, and having walked pointlessly around an empty field, we were back on the lane, which we now found to be similar in composition to a frozen river. I told Rob that this was his fault, if only for not stopping me from making the mistake in the first place.

Even Belle was having trouble maintaining her footing on the ice, and it was quite funny watching her legs splay this way and that until she finally figured out that if she walked on the fresh snow, it would be easier for her to keep upright.

I was busy enjoying one last giggle as her legs gave way when I missed my own footing and found myself heading towards the ground at an alarming speed, though I luckily landed in a snowdrift which completely broke my fall.

I quickly dragged myself up, and as Rob was a few yards ahead of me, he had no idea that I had just gone over, so luckily, this incident went unnoticed, although I then realized Belle was looking at me, and I'm sure she had at least a bit of a grin on her face.

The path turned to the left, following yet another dry-stone wall, and we could just make out a bit of a track. Rabbits darted this way and that, and Belle momentarily took chase, though she had no chance of catching anything at her age and in her condition. They say that dogs sometimes resemble their owners, and just like me, Belle had a bit of extra padding around her midriff, if you know what I mean. Just as I would never catch a rabbit, neither would she.

We were heading west now and into the wind, which blew hard on our faces. Every now and then, the wind would also whip up dry pieces of snow and ice, which then also blew painfully against us. The effect was probably similar to having your face sand-blasted, and although I have never taken part in such activities, of course, I can certainly imagine.

On top of this, the low-lying sun shone brilliantly in the still clear sky, and although I had sunglasses on, I still felt as if I was beginning to suffer from snow-blindness, so I was glad when the path finally began to turn to the north and away from the sun.

The route of the path wasn't clear at this point, particularly due to the fact that it was hidden between a thick layer of snow, so we just made our way around the mountain while trying to keep at the same height, as the map suggested the path did at this stage.

We would occasionally find ourselves back on a very clear path before almost immediately losing it again, and Belle simply made her own path. Once or twice, I found her sticking her head into big holes in the ground, presumably rabbit burrows, and had to shout for her to follow us, instructions which, quite surprisingly, she obeyed immediately.

I've already hinted that poor Belle can be a bit dim, and I didn't want her to get her head stuck in the ground, and I am being completely sincere when I say that. There are some things that she is good at and some that she is not, and rabbit catching is not her strong point.

She's not a very good dancer, either, though this makes sense when you consider that she has two left feet. Literally.

She is a very good guard dog, though, and her bark makes her sound like a big, vicious dog, rather than the window licking, bumble-bee eating, hedgehog sniffing fluff-ball that she actually is.

Every time someone rings the doorbell, though, she runs straight to the door and goes completely mental. And the thing is, I'm not even sure why she does this, as it's hardly ever for her.

At least dogs are brighter than cats. Our youngest cat, noodles, has a habit of jumping out of our window onto the roof of the porch below, or at least he did until he jumped out of it only to discover that we had demolished the porch the previous week. Don't worry, though, as just like all cats, he managed to land on his feet, although I'm pretty certain that he cashed in at least one of his nine lives that day.

Out of nowhere, we hit a wall, quite literally. The hill was very steep at this point, and we were on the western slopes of it, and to our left, any accident looked like it would end very badly indeed, possibly in a box around six feet under.

The wall in question ran before us in both directions, down to our left and up to our right, with seemingly no way through or over, being topped as it was by a bit of barbed wire. We surveyed it as far as we could see, but we agreed that there was no sign of a gate through it, so we did the only thing we could do, which was to start heading uphill. We figured there must be a gate somewhere over the brown of the hill, so we slowly trudged ever higher through the snowdrifts but still saw nothing.

We must have been somewhere near the top of the hill when, in the distance, we finally saw something which looked like a gate, and sure enough, when we got to it, we found ourselves back on the correct path. We later figured that we had turned too early after the farm, and had we been able to see the path under the thick snow, we would have gone the right way. I blame Rob.

This realisation led me to suggest to Rob that it might be more sensible to take the low route from Keld to Reeth today and leave the high route to another day. It had been hard work coming up

Kisdon Hill, and coupled with not being able to see the path, a change of plans seemed to be the most sensible thing to do. Rob agreed and suggested we decide fully when we got to Keld, where we could take a break in the pub and let the dog warm up in front of the fire for a half-hour or so, a plan which I suggested had only one flaw. Once we were in the pub, it would be hard to leave.

Once we were back on the path, the going was surprisingly good, and the track began to slowly head downhill.

Technically, we were now entering Swaledale, one of the most northerly and most beautiful of the Yorkshire Dales. Swaledale sits on the eastern side of the Pennines and runs from the Cumbria/Yorkshire border in the west more or less all the way to the beautiful market town of Richmond in the east. As we have already heard, the river that the valley gets its name from rises on the watershed in the far west, generally flowing towards the east through Keld, Thwaite, Muker and Reeth, before continuing on to meet the River Ure, and well, you know the rest.

Incidentally, the River Ure is said to be the home of a water beast. This beast is said to emerge soon after sunset before starting a hunt that lasts through the night. It only takes one human life a year, apparently, which is obviously good. It also usually emerges a lot further downstream than anywhere we had been near, which is also good, and it is said to live near Middleham.

Anyway, Swaledale runs parallel with Wensleydale, which we have, of course, just walked through east to west, though we will soon be going west to east in order to complete our great circle that is the James Herriot Way.

Historically, Swaledale has something of an industrial past, and we will at some point see the scars of various lead mines and other industries when we take the high route from Keld to Reeth, though again, it did not look like that would be happening today. Regardless, those days are now long gone, and today the area is primarily used for farming.

And lastly, although not as famous as Wensleydale cheese,

Swaledale also produces its own cheese. Like Wensleydale, this was originally made from ewe's milk, though it now comes from cows.

I suddenly received a reminder that today, the dale was like the arctic. A bitter wind blew from the west, bringing me straight back into the moment, but as we were now heading north, this was not so much of a problem and anyway, took only small amounts of skin from my face, with the resultant frostbite being classed as merely mild, in medical terms at least.

On a serious note, it was fascinating to watch the patterns of snow blowing around our feet, and every now and then, a surprisingly impressive vortex would create what looked like a mini-tornado swirling across the hillside towards us.

Belle was in her element once again, romping through the deep snowdrifts, though I did have to call her over once or twice to tighten up her coat which kept coming loose.

We came across an isolated cottage high on the hill to our right, and in the valley below, we could see the beginnings of Keld, which of course meant we would soon be warming up in the pub. I thought to myself that there are not many things better than walking into a nice welcoming pub, stomping the snow from your feet, and sitting down in front of a nice, roaring fire, and the more I thought of this, the more I looked forward to it. Belle was going to love it too.

Two children were enjoying sledging down a hill next to the cottage, which made me wonder if the snow was a rarity, even up here. As I said earlier, it had not been forecast, and as far as I was aware, there had not been much snow at all this winter, so if this was the case, we were doubly lucky. Although it was harder to walk in, the snow only added to the beauty of the dales, which was already immense, of course, and this made the extra effort more than worth it. As the children drew closer to us, slowly sliding down the hill, they had clearly seen Belle, and before I could do anything, she was running towards them and was soon enjoying rather a lot of attention from them as well.

Belle has an excellent temperament and is definitely used to being around children of all ages, and she certainly seems to enjoy their company. In fact, she enjoys the company of absolutely anyone so long as they stroke her and tickle her and generally make a fuss of her.

For some reason, watching these kids play with Belle reminded me of something funny my own son had once said about a dog, although I'm not sure why, as that situation was nothing like this one.

Many years before, my family and I were in town doing some shopping, and we happened to stop at the bank. Outside of the bank, for whatever reason, there was a police car parked up, and in the back of it was a rather large dog. A single policeman was leaning on the car, clearly deep in paperwork.

I then noticed that my young son, who was only around five years old at the time, had a puzzled look on his face, although I had no idea why. He was alternately staring at the policeman and the police car, and for some reason, he was clearly unable to make sense of what was going on. With that, he turned to the policeman and asked him if that was a dog in the back of the car. The policeman said that it was, which only caused my son to look even more puzzled. He thought for a moment longer, and then, with a completely straight face, he said to the policeman, *'what did he do?'*

As the path took a more determined downward aspect as we slowly headed into Swaledale, more of Keld village came into sight until I figured I could finally see the pub. However, it immediately dawned on me that there was no smoke coming from the chimney, and while the lack of a fire would certainly be a bit of disappointment, I was still looking forward to a rest, as I am sure Rob was too, although he was ahead of me at this stage. The view was staggering, and I was reminded of how James Herriot described passing from one dale to another as *an exquisite pleas-*

ure, and he was right.

Before we arrived in the village, we finally saw some sheep in a field to our right, and these were, in fact, Swaledale sheep. I don't just mean that they were here in Swaledale, but that was actually the name of their breed. I know we had seen them before, but somehow, it just seemed better to see Swaledales in actual Swaledale, but maybe that's just the big kid in me.

Apparently, the breed is bold and hardy, but considering what it is like up here in the depths of winter, it probably has to be. It is alert, which is always useful when you don't want to get eaten by something with pointy teeth, and the ewes are good lamb rearers too, or so they say. Even the wool is said to be of superior quality, more durable, and with an even texture having evolved in the frozen north, oh, and they also taste really, really nice when you pop one into the oven at gas mark six for an hour or two and chuck on a bit of mint sauce.

Swaledales are also pretty easy to spot. The upper parts of their faces are generally dark while the lower sections are white, and the old ones grow greyer with age, but then don't we all. All in all, if there was a top trumps card for a Swaledale sheep, it would have lots of points and would kick the crap out of lesser breeds such as a *Badger Faced Welsh Mountain Sheep* or even the truly ridiculous *Border Leicester*, which looks more like a rabbit it has to be said, or even the mean-looking *Beltex*, which if you imagine spray painting a pig to look like a sheep, well, that is exactly what a *Beltex* looks like, only nastier.

With Belle back on her lead for the first time in over an hour as she nervously watched the beasties to our right, we finally met the road that would soon take us into the village. It was devoid of traffic today, and only one car passed us by before we found ourselves at the war memorial, which was just a few yards from Keld Lodge.

As we approached, we were happy to see the door open, but soon enough, we realized that this had been an optical illusion, and it was, in fact, closed. Even worse, there was a note stuck on the door, and upon closer inspection, this note was, for us at least, a disaster. The note said the pub would be closed until the spring, which was a good few months away, and as I looked down at poor Belle, who was soggy and damp, I had to break the news that she would not be getting a pint after all. We, too, would have to wait for our hot chocolate, and also, of course, for any chance to warm up.

We wandered dejectedly back to the war memorial, which had just four names on it, and I noticed that the last name was Rukin, which was curious. We had stayed at the campsite down in the village on the Coast to Coast walk a few years earlier, and the owners of that were called Rukin, so it would be fair to assume that they are related. The next time I go, I shall ask, I decided.

After a minute or so, we moved on, down the steep road into Keld village itself, taking care over the slippery frozen tarmac that doubled as a ski slope today. I kept to the edge, and Belle followed, while Robin was a much braver man and wandered recklessly right down the middle. Unfortunately, much to my dismay, he completely failed to take part in any gymnastics on the way down, and even though I had my camera ready for any mishaps, this turned out to be a wholly wasted effort, and I froze my fingers for nothing.

The village was soon upon us, and we were pleased to find a self-service café which was apparently available for anyone to use. Even better, it had a defibrillator on the wall, which we would probably need quite soon, judging by how we were both huffing and puffing.

To the right of the café, by the way, is Birkshill View, a big old house where a man called Neddy Dick used to live. He was both well-known and well-loved in the dale, and he became quite famous for playing his lithophone, which is basically a musical instrument made of stones he had gathered from the river and is somewhat similar to a xylophone. It is said that Neddy was often reluctant to play music when asked but could be persuaded to do so by offering him a rabbit for barter and that when he did play, the sound was absolutely beautiful.

Sadly, Neddy died in 1926 and is now buried in Muker, and it is said that when he passed away, the stones of his instruments were ground down to dust and buried with him, which seems both a waste and a lot of effort to go to. Anyway, his fellow villagers loved him so much that one of them, Bob Pegg, even wrote a folk song to remember him by, which is called *The Ballad of Neddy Dick* and is actually quite good, at least it is if you like folk music.

While Rob waited outside with Belle, who was incredibly muddy, I popped into the cafe and made us both a coffee. After slipping some money into the honesty box, we were soon ready to go again, and after a conversation that lasted no more than five seconds, we unanimously confirmed our decision to take the low route today, as Kisdon Hill had put us completely off the idea of going up another mountain in these slippery and cold conditions. Belle agreed with us, apparently, as she had already wandered off down the path next to the river, so we did the only thing we could and followed after her.

Before we leave Keld, however, we should give it a few minutes more thought. I said earlier that Swaledale is now primarily a farming area, but tourism is also on the increase, mainly because it is one of the most beautiful places on earth, and Keld is at the heart of it.

In fact, Keld is perhaps one of the most important crossroads in the north of England. If you come here, however, there are no roundabouts or traffic lights or anything else to suggest its importance, but every year tens of thousands of people pass through here on either the Pennine Way or the Coast-to-Coast Path, although it should be said that most of them are sensible enough to come in the warmer months.

The 268-mile Pennine Way runs briefly through the dale south to north, and we have, of course, followed parts of it along our walk. On the other hand, Wainwright's 192-mile Coast to Coast runs through here west to east, with the paths crossing right here at Keld.

In case you've forgotten, The Pennine Way starts far south in Edale and slowly makes its way up the backbone of England, finishing just over the Scottish border at Kirk Yetholm in the beautiful Cheviot Hills, specifically at the Border Hotel where, if you remember, that free beer awaits all who successfully complete the mammoth walk. The Coast-to-Coast Path, on the other hand, devised by Alfred Wainwright, starts on the west coast of England at St Bees and finishes on the east coast at beautiful Robin Hood's Bay.

What this means, of course, is that every year thousands of walkers cross right here at Keld, sharing tales of leaky tents and blistered feet that all attempt to out-do one another, although in a purely friendly type of banter.

I have walked the Coast to Coast but have not yet tackled the Pennine Way, and whether I will ever get the chance to do it, I do not know, but I would certainly like to think that I will one day. When I do, I will be happy in the knowledge that hikers heading north out of Keld have the famous Tan Hill Inn as their next stopping point and watering hole. At 1,732 feet above sea level, this is not just the highest pub in England, but in the whole of the United Kingdom. It was famously cut off from the rest of the world in the harsh winter of 2010, and it must have been absolutely awful for those unlucky stranded visitors who then had to endure days of fine home-cooked food, real ales, and cosy fireside chats.

Anyway, in the meantime, then, I will have to settle for the best short long-distance footpath in the world, which is, of course, the Herriot Way, and which I am very much enjoying, as is Belle, looking at me with her big beautiful eyes as she is now, but maybe only because I am munching on a sausage roll which I then feel compelled to share with her. Well, it was those eyes, you see. I just couldn't say no.

There is also, however, one other, darker footpath that starts in Keld, and that would be the Swaledale Corpse Way. It is exactly as it sounds, and was previously the route that people would carry corpses along, and ran right through Swaledale to Grinton, which is where the nearest consecrated ground was located for a very long time, at least until St Mary's Church was built in Muker in the late 1500s.

The original 16-mile mediaeval track can still be followed today, and we will, in fact, be doing so ourselves now that we have decided on taking the low route. If you follow this path yourself, you will see various features along the way that could come in very useful indeed if you ever found yourself, and for whatever reason, I will not ask, also carrying a coffin through these beautiful hills. Several flat stones were placed along the route, and at Ivelet, just near the bridge, there is a particularly fine coffin stone where you can lay down your cadaver while you have a quick rest before crossing the River Swale, presumably reducing the chances of a splashy ending for anyone choosing to do so.

The route is, perhaps not surprisingly, somewhat steeped in folklore. It mostly avoids the villages on the way, which is in part down to Norse mythology, which states that the route is considered to mirror the last journey of the soul from the earth to the underworld and that settlements should be avoided lest they entice the dead to return, which would not be good, apparently. With this in mind, rituals and ceremonies were often performed at key places along the route, notably river crossings and crossroads, with the specific intention of preventing the dead from returning, though tales of ghostly happenings remained rife.

Shakespeare even had something to say about corpse roads, with Puck, a character in *A Midsummer Night's Dream*, talking of the dead following a particular path to their final resting place:

Now it is that time of night,

That the graves all gaping wide,

Every one lets forth his sprite,

In the church-way paths to glide.

Probably the most famous, or infamous story, come to think of it, is that of the headless black dog that many people have reported around here, having witnessed it jumping off the bridge at Ivelet into the River Swale, which is considered to be a bad omen and even a prophecy of doom and death. This is said to reflect a belief that river crossings were special in that spirits could not cross water, which, of course, begs the question of the need for those ceremonies in the first place. Maybe they were just making sure and wanted to be a hundred per cent certain that the in-laws would never be back. Either way, don't say you haven't been warned.

And lastly on this subject, corpse roads, in general, can be quite hard to navigate. We have already heard how they tended to avoid settlements, but they also often traversed the most remote and difficult terrain possible. This was often deliberate, as landowners did not want these routes to become rights of way, so they became paths you would use only if you really had to.

Two last things on Swaledale, at least for now. The first is that the dale is home to the famous Yorkshire Shepherdess Amanda Owen. You will perhaps know who I mean when I say her of many children who lives on a farm and who we, in fact, met while walking the Coast-to-Coast a few years back. She probably has even more kids now, but even back then, the little things were running all over the place, as well they should. And they were all incredibly polite. She runs a tea shop a short distance away up at Ravenseat, and in the interest of supporting the local economy, you should pop in for tea and scones, assuming you can manage the extra mileage, that is.

The second thing is that famous writer Wystan Hugh Auden, much better known of course as WH Auden, famous for his *Funeral Blues* poem where he suggests we *stop all the clocks and prevent the dog from barking with a big juicy bone*, which became even more famous after the sad funeral scene in *Four Weddings and a Funeral*, once described the heart of the Pennines around Swaledale as his *great good place*. He was right, because it is.

Anyway, we followed Belle along the path, which soon had us next to the riverbank. The sound of the River Swale had gradually grown louder, and when it had finally come into sight, we could see an impressive waterfall on the opposite bank. At first, I thought it was Kisdon Force, a rather famous waterfall around here, but I quickly realized it was actually East Gill Force, and today it was very impressive and in full flow, spewing hundreds of gallons of water into the River Swale every second. Seeing Kisdon Force would have to wait until we followed the high route after all, apparently.

On the northeast side of Kisdon Hill, just up ahead of us, is an area called Hartlakes. For whatever reason, this is a place that is said to be haunted, and one house, in particular, Boggle House, has even been described as one of the most haunted houses in the country. Quite worryingly, boggle is also an old word used to describe a wandering ghost or spirit, so we probably won't be hanging around as we pass through.

Boggle House, then, was once home to John Alton and his family, though he was also commonly known as Snapper John. One day, while he and his wife were away visiting the market in nearby Muker, his daughter managed to set her clothes on fire. It was said at the time that the girl leapt up and down in such agony from floor to ceiling that she even left marks where her head hit the roof.

Snapper John and his wife remained in the house after the tragic death of their beloved daughter, but soon enough, strange sounds began to haunt them at night until they could stand it no more and fled in terror, never to return. No one has lived in the house ever since these tragic events, and even the locals avoid it, especially at night.

The path continued to snake through a small woodland that was very pretty and reminded me of an enchanted forest, or possibly something out of *The Lord of The Rings*. It was almost rainforest like, and as the path led this way and that, up and over several small hills, I was keeping a sharp eye out for Boggle House.

We found it soon enough, though it is just a ruin nowadays, and while I took a picture of it, I felt no inclination to go inside. I'm not usually superstitious, but I just felt the need to keep away. I did suggest that Rob stick his head in, but again, he didn't seem too keen, the chicken.

The path soon opened up into pleasant meadows, where we bumped into the first walkers we had come across today. They were coming from the opposite direction, and there were three of them, and I presumed them to be husband, wife and son. The youngster kept quiet, but we had a good chat with the parents, if that is who they were, of course.

They said they had come from Muker, though I think they pronounced it wrong, but what do I know? They had said it is pronounced as Mucker, though I am told it is supposed to be pronounced the same way as a cat mews.

Anyway, it had taken them about an hour to get here, too, they added, which was a surprisingly long time for what was only a couple of miles, though they quickly added that they had stopped to take lots of photographs.

They also told us that there was another couple ahead of us, somewhat older, who could possibly be the couple that had been on our bus, as they had asked for tickets to Keld and would therefore be ahead of us, presumably.

After a brief but informative chat, we plodded on, at which point my paper map blew away. I ran down a steep bank to get it before it went into the river, slipping on my side in the process. As Belle and Rob eyed me pathetically, with more than a hint of a smile, I should add, I finally caught up with it and managed to get a foot on it before it blew even further away.

Although it was only a map that I had printed myself at home, I was happy to retrieve it, but then realized my folly. I had printed off the map for the higher route, and as we were now taking the lower route, this map was effectively useless. Not that you could really see it anymore, however, due to the rather large, size nine footprint that covered most of it, and which was particularly blocking out the important bits.

We plodded on across the meadow, with several large puddles that caused continuous minor detours, most of which were frozen over. The sun was beginning to come over the brow of the hills to the east, which would soon start to melt these puddles, I pondered, which might make our paths a bit wet later on.

We followed the River Swale downstream for a while, and again Belle was off her lead as all of the sheep had vanished, presumably to somewhere warmer. The river was wide and rocky at this point and had the look of a proper mountain stream. Several abandoned cow houses dotted the landscape, for that is what they called barns around here, and one was more impressive than the others, and it might even have been a proper house. Whoever built it had seemingly done a good job, as it was more or less intact, although it did appear to be on what was now a floodplain.

In the distance, we caught our first glimpse of Ramps Holme Bridge, which we would need to cross soon enough. The River Swale has a reputation for sudden floods and has washed several bridges away over the years, but whoever built this bridge had that exact eventuality in mind. They had built the bridge extremely high above the water and had constructed huge foundations which would not be easy to wash away. Every time the river floods, by the way, there is another positive side-effect. The meadows here are an abundance of wildflowers in the spring and the summer, and it is the flooding that makes this possible by giving the soil a rich cocktail of nutrients, resulting in a yellow carpet of flowers year after year, including some rarer types such as the butterfly orchid and the burnt mantle orchid. The flowers, in turn, attract a plethora of insects, which themselves serve to attract a rich variety of birds.

Today, however, the only carpet is white, so we carry on, heading towards the bridge, with not a soul in sight.

Unfortunately, and I am going to have to blame Rob for this, we then got lost. I suggested to Rob that we stay on the main path, which appeared to be going uphill and into the woods, but this was the wrong way. Considering that Rob never corrected me, it is, therefore, factually correct that it was his fault that we got lost.

We had actually been heading towards Muker and had to turn around, and although we were not visiting the place today, it is only a short walk should you need refreshments, and it is also worth giving the village five minutes of our time within these pages.

Muker, you see, was, in fact, supposedly the place where the first sighting of a wild flamingo in Britain was made, way back in the mid-1800s. Of course, such an exotic and interesting sighting caused much excitement in the village and beyond, and in typical Yorkshire fashion, the locals did the only thing they could; they cooked it. Not surprisingly, perhaps, it was reported that it tasted a bit like chicken.

The place is said to be somewhat haunted, too, with several accounts of spooky happenings over the years. For instance, in the early 1800s, a man called Kit Brunskill moved in with his female cousin, but shortly after, she inexplicably hanged herself in the kitchen. She was apparently jealous of him and did such a good job of doing herself in that her head became detached from her trunk and was hastily buried in a box at midnight in the churchyard, an act which probably raises more questions than it answers, when you think about it. Anyway, ever since, there have been occasional sightings of this headless spectre around the village, although presumably most of these have occurred just after closing time at the local pub.

An even more spooky story surrounds an old schoolmaster who resided in the village, also in the mid-1800s, which was recounted in the Leeds Mercury in 1897. Raymond, as he was known, was a particularly cruel man who would have his students pointlessly reciting verses at their desks while he daubed away at pictures. When he vanished, then, and was later found ever so slightly dead, there was perhaps not a lot of sadness about his passing, though the circumstances within which the events occurred certainly attracted considerable interest at the time.

As well as being the schoolmaster, you see, Raymond also kept a couple of cattle just outside the village, and whenever he went to tend to them, he always had to pass a cow house at Pith Hill, which was reputed to be haunted. The ghosts in question were fiendish imps, who were said to terrorise the entire dale with their unearthly choir.

So it was, one dark and stormy night, that the imps ambushed poor Raymond by jumping from the cow house and almost giving him a heart attack. Not having a defibrillator, he ran back to Muker in double-time, and it was a few days before he plucked up enough courage to attempt a return. He was forced to do this, though, due to the needs of his cows, and he was now more determined than ever to bring them nearer to his home so he could avoid the spooky spectres on subsequent trips.

He set out at nightfall, but when he had not returned by the next morning, a search was organized, and in short order, poor Raymond was soon found. Unfortunately, by the time they found him, he was as dead as a dodo and as stiff as a brush and was found lying between two of his cattle.

Although no one ever found out exactly how poor Raymond died, it was said at the time that the imps chased him to his death, and Pith Hill cow house is still a spot to be avoided even to this day, particularly on a dark night. It is said that the place requires more courage than even a six-foot man can muster, so I've got no chance, though Rob might. Rob, you see, is very tall indeed. And lastly, every now and then, the unearthly choir of the imps can still be heard haunting the dale, though again, this is usually after last orders at the pub.

Anyway, back to our walk. We should actually have stayed as close to the river as possible on our approach to the bridge rather than going up the hill. Had we done so, we would have seen the path, which although it looked as if it disappeared ahead of us, it did not, though it did become very narrow. Anyway, after going back down the hill and briefly walking along the well-built path that hugged the river ever so tightly, we finally got to the bridge, and Belle was at the front.

Unfortunately, the bridge was very narrow, and although Belle had gone ahead, she was clearly not enjoying crossing it. She was taking baby steps, her tail had dropped between her back legs, and she was very low to the ground. I had never seen her like this before, basically terrified, but after catching up with her and giving her some words of encouragement – words such as chew stick and biscuit - she finally made it across.

We next hugged the north bank of the river, still generally heading east with the bright sunlight no longer blinding us, thankfully. The meadows and fields continued, and in one or two, we found the odd sheep which all eyed Belle suspiciously. In one particularly large field, a rather bullish-looking ram approached her, and for a minute, I thought he was going to charge. I was ready to let go of her lead so she could run away, but the ram seemingly changed his mind at the last minute. Nonetheless, we left that field rather quickly.

High up on the hill to our left was a farmstead known locally as Calvert Houses. Behind it is an area with perhaps a more interesting name than the dungeon had, for an empty patch of grass up there is known as Puke's Field. I had wondered if it was maybe named after a particularly rambunctious New Year's Eve party or perhaps a wedding that had gotten a bit out of hand, but apparently, Puke's is the shortened version of the surname Peacock, which is quite common around here. Anyway, I mention it as this is also where a rabid dog was finally cornered and killed after going on a rampage across Swaledale way back in 1871, but more of that later.

After another mile or so of the same pleasant meadows, we finally came to a small road and, with it, the first hint of civilization. We knew Ivelet was not far ahead of us, which was confirmed when we came to the impressive bridge just before the village, and after a brief chat, we decided to stop in the village at whatever café or pub was open, no matter how expensive it might be.

The bridge, by the way, was incredibly pretty to look at, being built with one huge archway back in 1687 and which, when the conditions are right, reflects in the water forming an almost perfect circle. The bridge is also a reminder that we are still on the corpse way, as at the north end on the floor, you can see one of those coffin stones we heard of earlier, where mourners would place their loved ones down for a while in order to rest. If you remember, this is also the bridge where the headless black dog can be seen jumping into the water, and if you ever see it yourself, you should start saying your final prayers.

Luckily there was only one dog around today, and that was Belle, and she definitely had a head, although I sometimes wondered if it was empty. Don't get me wrong, she's a lovely dog, but there is no easy way to say that she is sometimes a bit dim. For instance, when she was a puppy, she once took all of her toys over to the mirror so the 'other' dog could play with them. And if that's not an indication of her general level of intelligence, I can fondly recall the time when I took her for a walk in the fields behind our house. It was a fine, sunny day, and I had taken her favourite ball for her to play with, but on the first throw, she ran after it, only to come back with a potato. I wouldn't mind, but the ball was yellow, and the potato was, well, potato-coloured. It wasn't even round, and we never did see that ball again. And before you tell me that dogs are colour blind, well, that is sort of true, but it has been misconstrued by many people over the years to the point where large numbers of people actually believe that dogs can only see in black and white, which is complete and utter nonsense.

When it comes to dogs, you see, we should consider them to have colour vision deficiency rather than being full-on colour blind. In fact, dogs see in a very similar way to that which many humans with red-green colour blindness are able to see. In all of our eyes, whether you are a human or a dog, we have receptors that allow us to see colour and these are called cones. Most humans have three sets of cones in their eyes, which roughly correspond to the colours red, green and blue-violet. The combination of these three types of colour receptors, therefore, allows us to see an incredibly wide spectrum of light, up to around one million colours. Interestingly, there have been cases reported where some lucky people have a fourth cone, and it is thought that they can see around a hundred million colours, which must be both cool and freaky at the same time.

Dogs, on the other hand, have only two sets of cones, and these roughly correspond to the colours blue and yellow, which means that dogs see a much narrower spectrum of colours compared to us. Well, actually, thinking about it, not us at all, as I myself suffer from colour blindness, so I can probably only see about as well as Belle. Anyway, the point I am trying to make is that she had no excuses for not seeing that yellow ball, hence why I am wondering if she has an empty head.

On another occasion, she managed to dye herself green after following me around the garden while I cut the grass, but the biggest indication of her intelligence is that, even after ten years of living with us, she still sits staring at a picture on our wall thinking it is a window.

She's gotten herself into trouble once or twice, too. I came home to a messy kitchen one day, and it was obvious that one of our animals had raked through the bin in search of snacks. I wondered which one of them it might have been, but luckily there was a rather big clue. Belle was asleep at the bottom of the bin.

The best example, though, of her being a dog of very little brain, is the story of the sausage. Around five years ago, on one of our more regular walks, Belle managed to schnaffle a sausage from under a bush. I tried to get it off her, but I was too slow, and she swallowed the whole thing in one go. Now, every time we go on this same walk, she has to religiously check this apparently magic sausage bush, just in case. She does it every time.

Anyway, we moved off into the village in search of refreshments, so how disappointed were we, then, when the village turned out to have nothing in the way of, well, anything at all really. Just a few houses dotted the roadside, and we had left the place more or less before we knew we had even arrived as a sign next to the phone box led us on our way. We would just have to wait for Gunnerside, we decided, and pray for a café or a pub, though of course, we had no choice in the matter anyway.

Back into the fields we went, with Belle once again running free. The path, at least, was fairly obvious at this point, as some other people had presumably been along it earlier on and had left a trail of snowy footprints. We went from field to field, once again navigating directly to the next obvious gate, and at some point, we caught sight of three figures ahead of us. We almost caught them up just before Gunnerside, and in fact, we would have had I not slipped on some ice and then immediately hit the floor like a brick. I picked myself up straight away, but it was too late, as everyone had heard my rather high-pitched scream and had presumably turned around expecting to see maybe a young child or perhaps a howler monkey.

Rob had done the exact same thing just a few minutes back, minus the scream, of course, but with the addition of some rather interesting and unprintable words, and while he said that he had hurt his ankle, I felt no pain, at least not initially. However, after less than a minute, I began to feel a sharp pain in my right knee and ankle. I bravely decided to walk it off, I told Rob, who rolled his eyes and ignored me, although on a serious note for just a minute, I did briefly think I had done some serious damage.

Pain shot up my leg with every step, which is unfortunate when you are on a walk of around forty thousand or so of them. Still, I plodded on, now limping, and told myself that I would walk it off.

With Gunnerside now in sight, the people ahead of us had vanished, which at least meant I would not have to explain my scream, and as the path began to drop down the hill, I felt the pain in my knee and ankle recede somewhat, which was good.

Walking into Gunnerside, it seemed as if we were walking through someone's garden, which we probably were. They had lots of garden ornaments and lights on display, and it was all very pretty, but the real delight came around the corner, in the village proper.

In the garden of a fine stone cottage, someone had put up a signpost pointing to, among other places, Beverley, as well as to the local pub. Beverley is a small town close to where Rob and I live, and I was just commenting on this when I heard a loud laugh from the side of the house. A lady emerged, and we immediately struck up a conversation, and it turned out that it was her husband who was from Beverley. They had just retired here after spending a couple of years renovating the house.

They had done a good job, too, and I asked about the pub and whether or not it was open. Alas, the news was not good, and the pub was never open on a Tuesday, apparently. I thought this odd, but her husband, who had now joined us after presumably looking outside and wondering why two tramps were chatting up his wife, said that the villagers had recently bought the pub between them and were working hard to get it up and running properly.

He did tell us that there were benches in the village where we could stop for our lunch, so after bidding them farewell and leaving them to their day, we moved on.

We did indeed find some benches on a small traffic island, but we could also see the pub, and figuring that it would have picnic benches, we headed to that instead.

The benches were wet, though, so we remained standing, but Rob produced a flask of coffee while I fed Belle a full tin of the finest doggy slop available. After this, I devoured my own sandwiches in short order while I stared at the beautiful mountain to the north, which was presumably Gunnerside Moor.

Historically, Gunnerside Moor was supposed to be the home of devilish goblins called trows. Although much more common up in the Shetland and the Orkney Islands off the coast of Scotland, they were also thought to inhabit the hills and ancient mounds around here and were said to be somewhat similar to Norwegian trolls. The archetypal trow was said to be an ugly, mischievous little creature, and although some were said to be able to pass as a man, it was generally one that was old, wizened or even possibly deformed, which seems a bit harsh. They were nocturnal and never appeared during the daylight, which reminds me of my friend Chris, and even when they emerged at night, they were invisible to most. Trows probably have Viking origins, which would certainly help to explain their presence here, as Vikings regularly ventured south to these Yorkshire Dales for a nice bit of pillaging, often targeting early Christian monasteries that provided soft targets that contained great wealth, and thus basically became the equivalent of a cash machine for the Viking raiders.

All of this reminded me of a time when I met a man who

matched the description of a trow a few years ago, while we had been mid-way through our Coast to Coast Walk, which of course passes through the very same hills and dales we now found ourselves walking through on the Herriot Way. This specific encounter had happened at Keld Lodge, just a couple of miles back, and which was and remains a fine old stone-built pub, even if it is closed until spring. The man in question was of hobbit-like proportions with a long wizard-like beard and who, when we met him, was completely wasted. When I spoke to him, he didn't know where he was or where he was going. He had no idea where he was staying either, and this is the most bizarre bit; he completely vanished despite never having appeared to have left the pub. Perhaps he was a trow?

Anyway, back to today, and what tends to happen when you are outside, is that your body begins to cool quite rapidly as soon as you stop walking. So it was that after only a few minutes, we were once again off on our way, although we now had rather full bellies.

Belle soon developed a new lease of life, and as we headed out of Gunnerside up a steep hill, she was immediately off and far ahead of us while we both lagged lazily behind. Halfway up this hill, we came across an old abandoned house, which we remembered from our Coast-to-Coast walk, as this section of the Herriot Way still shared the same route for a few miles more. This was also the old Corpse Way, and I mentioned to Rob that I could not imagine carrying a coffin over these hills, and in fact, I could barely carry myself.

Passing through a couple of small woods and then a farm, we soon found ourselves at the top of a plateau that spread out before us in a manner similar to what I imagined Siberia to look like. A frozen landscape beckoned us, and although it was almost featureless in the whiteout of today, we could just about make out the line of what we presumed to be our path.

Belle again shot off in all directions while I followed Rob, literally in his footsteps. The snow was even thicker up here, so it was helpful that he was leaving rather large holes for me to step into, although being the giant that he was, I was having difficulty getting from one hole to the next as they were pretty well spaced out for a shortie like me.

The path followed the southern edge of Great Rowleth, although, at some point, we appeared to have gone much higher than we had intended to, ending up on a rather amusingly named hill simply called Barf. We should have stayed much lower, but once again, it had been impossible to see the path, and anyway, it was Rob's fault.

We got our heads down and moved on, with an apparent blizzard blowing all around us, and although we had only climbed to a height of around 1,000 feet or so, the difference in conditions up here was astounding. I was glad I was wearing thermals and had also remembered to bring gloves and a hat, yet once again, I looked at Belle in awe as she did not seem to be bothered by the conditions in the slightest.

When we finally saw Isles Bridge in the valley far below us, we realized our mistake and decided we had better begin heading down towards it. The path zigged and zagged and was generally pretty good, with the only hairy bit being when we crossed a small waterfall, which Rob did by jumping precariously from rock to rock. It was actually pretty dangerous, and one false move would have seen him going towards a splashy and messy outcome, and probably certain death, so I waited until he was safely across, which is when Belle and myself used the gate behind a wall that Rob had missed. I'm not sure what the look was that he gave me exactly, but it was not a good one.

We continued downhill, somehow ending up exactly where we wanted to be, though neither of us knew how we had managed it. One last zig and zag had us finally at Isles Bridge, where we crossed over the River Swale once more, and here it was even wider than it had been further upstream and just as fast.

Turning east once again, Belle was beginning to show signs of fatigue, judging by how closely she was now following Rob and myself. She was no longer running this way and that, and when I looked her in the eye, I saw the same tiredness in her that I felt myself.

The road here was potholed and wet. With the sun now dropping below the hills behind us, I sensed that the ground was slowly beginning to freeze again, and this was confirmed when Rob suddenly squealed out like a child and did a quick windmill impression. I was just pulling my camera out so I could take a picture of him sprawled out across the floor when, unfortunately, he regained his balance and, much to my disappointment, never fell after all.

The road turned into a track, which I suspect was yet another part of the Corpse Way, which was quite fitting as that was more or less the condition that we were all now in. We were done in; both of us had had enough of walking, and we were now actively counting down the miles to Reeth. We reckoned it was no more than four miles, which made it an hour away, which was good as that was also about the same amount of daylight we had left. Unfortunately for Belle, four human miles is about twenty doggy miles, though I was not cruel enough to tell her this.

We passed How Hill, which is actually an old iron age fort, just before Scabba Wath Bridge, which is an awesome name for a bridge. How Hill looked just like a prominent hill, and there was no sign of a fort today, and the only thing that gave it away as being artificial, in my eyes anyway, was its uniform shape and the fact that it stuck out like a sore thumb.

Just past this bridge, on the other side of the river, is a small village called Healaugh, pronounced *hee-law*, although, for some reason, probably related to hypothermia and the early onset of madness, Rob kept calling it *hallelujah*.

There was another fort high on the hill to our right, though I could see no sign of it as I looked. This would be Maiden Castle, and it is said to date from the iron age, which means that it is from around 600 BC, which is pretty amazing, and the name is perhaps one of the more interesting points about the place anyway. Maiden in this sense means virgin, and in the sense of the castle, it supposedly means one that has never been taken in battle, which makes perfect sense when you think about it, although some experts are adamant that the earthworks were never meant to be defensive in nature, but were probably just ceremonial. Whatever the truth is, the hillfort is unusual in that it is the only one of its type known to have a long, processional entrance made of stone.

Legends surround the hillfort, and it is said by some that there is buried treasure somewhere within its bounds. Even better, this treasure is supposedly a chest of gold, according to one William Henderson anyway, who wrote in 1879 that some local men finally managed to find the treasure, only to be chased away, first by a chicken, and secondly by a thunderstorm. I suspect, a bit like all those who have witnessed ghosts around these parts over the years, these men had also been to the pub at some point, but who am I to judge?

It is still said to be haunted, get this, by a magic hen, presumably the one that scared away the Victorians. And apparently, there is indeed a hoard of treasure buried somewhere in the castle, though all attempts to find it are doomed to failure for all eternity. The magic hen can extinguish all flames, you see, thereby making it impossible for you to find your way around unless, that is, you come during the day. However, if you do that, then the hen will summon up a storm to get rid of you instead, or so the legend goes.

We carried on along the track, which soon turned into a muddy path much to Belle's delight, and followed the river's course for the last couple of miles. The sheep were still out here, which meant Belle was back on her lead, at least for a while, and eventually, Rob announced that he could see the suspension bridge that would lead us into Reeth.

I looked to where he pointed but saw nothing and assumed him to be tripping, but a few minutes later, I too could see it and realized that I was just a bit less observant than he was and had poorer eyesight.

I wanted to keep Belle on her lead as much as possible now, given that we were nearing the end of the walk and would once again be crossing roads with at least some traffic on them, but she clearly wanted to be off and about. I often wondered what would happen if she managed to get lost out here, and although she has a microchip fitted, it would be my worst nightmare come true. It was well over a hundred miles to my house, and although I had heard of many stories of dogs crossing tremendous distances in order to get back to their owners, I really didn't ever want to be in that situation.

On this note, one of the most interesting stores of dogs making their way back to their owners is that of a small Irish Terrier called Prince, which is astounding because this wasn't your average story of a dog simply making its way home. Prince was the dog of a man called James Brown, who acquired him while he was posted to Ireland with the army in 1913. In 1914, at the onset of the First World War, Prince was sent to the family home in London while Brown was shipped off to the trenches of France.

However, after only a month, the little dog went missing, and although his loss was reported to the local police, he was presumed lost forever. Mrs Brown wrote to Mr brown detailing the sad news, and everyone was presumably sad for a while, until one day, Prince somehow quite miraculously turned up in the battlefields of France after being missing for around two months.

Although this story seems absolutely impossible and incredibly far-fetched, it was thoroughly investigated by the Royal Society for the Protection of Animals (RSPCA) at the time and was widely reported in both the local and national press.

Anyway, after the somewhat awkward experience of explaining this incident to his commanding officer, Brown saw his little dog become the regimental mascot, and I am glad to say that both of them managed to survive the war, despite seeing action at both Passchendaele and Vimy Ridge. However, the end of the war brought a new problem, that of getting Prince back to England, as technically he had never left.

Luckily, once again, the RSPCA stepped in and housed Prince throughout his six-month quarantine, after which he went straight back to the family home and lived happily ever after.

I am always amazed when I hear of dogs managing to cover great distances in order to get home, but that one is particularly fascinating because nobody ever figured out how Prince managed to travel to and find his owner hundreds of miles away from home, not only in a foreign country but across the English Channel.

There was no chance of this with Belle today, anyway, as she was now literally stuck to us like glue as we walked along the edge of the river, and this was presumably because she was incredibly tired, just like us.

The river meandered this way and that, which cruelly added further miles to our walk, but soon enough, we found ourselves crossing one final field and heading for the bridge. The lights of Reeth could be seen twinkling gently in the distance, and we knew we were nearly done, hopefully with a log fire and a pub as our reward.

This small pedestrian bridge that next takes us into Reeth is actually known locally as the Reeth Swing Bridge, but an initial and cursory examination soon suggests that it is most definitely a suspension bridge and not a swing bridge at all. However, this bridge is a replacement and was built after the original, which dated from 1920, was destroyed by a fallen tree in 2000, and it is the original to which the name Swing Bridge really applies. Back in the day, you see, local children on their way to school from the farms of Harkerside on the south bank of the River Swale would often gather in large numbers and make the bridge swing wildly from side to side. Ah, the good old days before health and safety spoilt all our fun.

I must admit that when I crossed this bridge, I did give it a little swing or two, but Belle was not impressed, so I gave up on the idea of making it swing properly and was soon at the other side. Belle still gave me a dirty look, however. She had actually struggled to cross it once again and had lowered her body and hobbled slowly across, just like she did at Ramps Holme Bridge earlier on, with her tail stuck in between her back legs again despite this bridge being much bigger than the last. Eventually, she made it across despite my antics, which meant we had almost finished our walk.

Or maybe we hadn't. Unfortunately, events then conspired against us; heading down the path towards Reeth, we soon came to a fence where a sign had been erected, which announced a temporary diversion due to path erosion. The diversion looked pretty meaty, too, and would lead us a considerable distance in the opposite direction before bringing us back around and into the village, which at this stage was only a few hundred feet to our north and was clearly visible. This would, of course, add unwelcome mileage to our walk at a very late stage indeed.

I suggested to Rob that the diversion could go and fish, and as long as we were careful, we could manage a little bit of path erosion. Rob didn't look so sure, so I said I would go and check the condition of the path ahead in order to save him what might be a pointless walk there and back.

Instructing Belle to stay with Rob, I set off on my way, but after only a few seconds, I could hear panting directly behind me. Luckily, it wasn't Rob, though I had no idea how Belle had managed to get through the narrow fence, especially bearing in mind the difficulties she had encountered with those squeeze gates all day long. Nonetheless, here she was.

We carried on, almost there, and when we got there, we discovered that *there* had gone. What I mean is that not only had the path gone, but the grass was gone, the riverbank was gone, and the ground was gone. The River Swale, famous as it is, of course for washing things away and being one of the fastest rivers in England, had certainly done its job here, and there was literally no way to continue.

Below me was a mass of swirling, muddy water, and as I watched it, I could actually see bits of riverbank breaking off and falling into the water right before my eyes. The river was literally changing course before me, and when I later looked at a map, it would appear that it was slowly moving north. This may sound odd, but we have to remember that rivers do this, and although we might look at the natural world around us and assume things have always been as they are, this could not be further from the truth. We humans have little idea of geological time with our incredibly short lifespan, but then how could we?

I wandered back to Rob and explained that not only had the path gone, but the ground had gone, so we would have no alternative other than to follow the diversion shown on the sign, which I took a quick photo of, just in case we got lost, which let's face it, was quite likely.

The darkness was becoming quite apparent by now, and although we could still just about see, it would soon be pitch black, so without further ado, we wandered off, but obviously not in the direction we wanted to go.

In fairness, it wasn't a long diversion, and it was certainly better than falling into an icy river and dying a terrible death. I'm not sure about you, but I want to die a nice death, if you get my meaning. Drowning must be awful, as must dying by fire. No, I want to die nice and peacefully in my sleep, like my grandad, and not screaming out in terror, like his passengers.

The detour probably added no more than a mile to our walk, and surprisingly, we didn't get lost, and as we wandered into the outskirts of Reeth, we looked around, hoping to find a nice warm pub with some lights on. The first one, the Buck Hotel, seemed shrouded in darkness, but the second and third were both open. The Kings Arms looked very welcoming, as did the Black Bull next door, so I left it up to Rob to choose which one we would grace with our presence and our pennies.

He decided on the Kings Arms because it was closer, which made me laugh because we were parked directly opposite both of them, and the difference in distance was negligible. When you have walked eighteen miles, though, Rob explained in all seriousness, every step counts, and I think he actually meant it.

We dumped our stuff in the car, grabbed our clean shoes to change into, and ventured into the pub. I had wondered if they were dog friendly, but as we went in, a rather large greyhound behind the bar suggested they were. Don't get me wrong, the greyhound wasn't working there; I mean, what would a dog be doing working in a pub. I imagine he was just a customer.

As the couple who owned him put him back on his lead and left the pub, Belle became the only dog in there, and when she saw a roaring fire at the far end of the pub, she was off. It didn't matter that a couple of people were already sitting in front of the fire, as she simply inserted herself between them and the warmth and promptly collapsed. I am seriously going to have to teach that dog some manners, I thought to myself.

Rob went to get us a drink while I grabbed a table in the corner and as near to the fire as possible without actually stealing someone else's table, taking my muddy boots off while I waited. By now, Belle was snoring and probably farting in her sleep, but she looked comfortable nonetheless, although she did seem a little too close to the fire than would seem sensible. She tends to do that, which is to say she will sit far too close until she gets too hot and will then move away. Later, she will move closer again and then repeat this pattern all night.

When I had taken my shoes off, I was surprised to find my feet totally dry. The shoes I had on today were brand new and were not even worn in, though they didn't need to be as they were made by Meindl. I don't work for them, and they did not pay me, and indeed I had to buy these shoes at the full retail price just a week or so ago, so I have no vested interest here, but these really are good shoes.

My other shoes had been comfortable enough, but even though they had been advertised as waterproof, I had always ended up with wet feet while wearing them in wet weather. That these shoes had been through snowdrifts and puddles today yet had remained completely dry was a good sign indeed, although they were still just a little bit smelly. Still, I expect there is not much you could do about that as they had had my stinky feet in them all day.

I was interrupted from admiring my dry but somewhat aromatic feet by a man who was for some reason dressed as a chef. It turned out that he was indeed a chef, and had brought Belle a meaty platter. It was a big one too and was composed of dog biscuits, sliced ham, a bit of beef and even some black pudding. I thanked him profusely for his very kind gesture, and Belle's eyes nearly popped out of her head when she saw it. She had soon devoured every morsel of her surprise snack, and I half expected her to burp, but instead, she just lay down and went back to sleep in front of the fire. I could have done with one of those myself, I thought, as I had watched her eat that meaty feast.

Rob returned with our drinks, and we soon got talking to the couple that Belle had so rudely sat in front of. They were staying here, at the Kings Arms, they said, and were enjoying it immensely, although they did mention that they had been at least a little colder ever since my fat dog had arrived. When they found out that we were from Hull, the gentleman, if I can call him that, spent the rest of the conversation making fun of our beloved hometown and even suggested at one point that some of my relatives might be related a bit too closely, if you know what I mean, but he did it in such a funny manner that I decided not to murder him and bury him behind the pub or chuck him in the river.

I think he was some kind of comedian, and he had said that he was also a disc jockey on occasion, but all in all, he rounded off our day in such a good manner, that in retrospect, I could not have imagined a better way for it to end.

ROUND AND BACK AGAIN

Reeth to Aysgarth

We started today much the same as the last stretch with a drive to Reeth; however, we left Rob's car in Aysgarth as, once again, it is problematic to get from one to the other without the ability to teleport, and a taxi was even more unlikely due to the cost. We could have booked the little white bus, but that would have required the ability to plan, which we clearly do not have, despite having the appearance at least of being adults.

Adulthood is overrated anyway, as you have to do everything yourself, and even worse than that, people no longer care what your favourite dinosaur is. Don't get me wrong, being an adult definitely has its advantages, but I do have many memories from my childhood that I am very fond of. My favourite childhood memory, for instance, is my knees not hurting. Nowadays, I wake up every morning wondering if I am coming down with one illness or another or if this is just how I wake up now. Also, adulthood can basically be described as making an involuntary grunt every time you do anything involving some kind of movement, which I only realized when my kids pointed it out and compared me to a chimp.

Your lifestyle changes too. I vividly remember sneaking out of the house by climbing through my bedroom window, usually destined for a party. Nowadays, I am more likely to be found sneaking out of parties to go back to my house, though I usually use the door these days and not the window.

Not that all of my decisions growing up have been good ones, though. Regardless, I have a philosophy that says how bad can any of your decisions be if no one has come from the future to stop you from doing it? You have to admit that this makes sense. And by the way, my favourite dinosaur is a diplodocus, on the basis that it is the least likely to eat a chubby old hiker, not that anybody cares, of course.

While we are on this subject, it would appear that I am not the only adult that has not quite grown up. Rob told me that recent government figures suggest that certain types of accidents increased during the last couple of years. For instance, over five thousand people ended up in hospital after falls from playground equipment such as swings and slides. You would think that these people would all be children, but this is not so, and hundreds of adults were among those hospitalized.

Further figures tell us, for instance, that thousands more ended up seeking medical attention following accidents with hand tools such as hammers and saws, and hundreds reportedly turned up at emergency rooms after being injured by lawnmowers, though hopefully not all at once. And in among those statistics is a 90-year-old woman who was injured by a crocodile. Whatever she was doing, I do hope it was worth it. The only conclusion from all of this, then, is that we are slowly becoming more stupid as a population.

Anyway, enough of that, as we really had to move on. Today was certainly different to last time in at least one respect, which was the weather. Most of the snow had melted away, and only isolated pockets remained on the highest peaks, and even then, only on the most shaded sides.

The warmer weather, and I use the word warmer only in the sense that everything was not quite as frozen as it had been before, also meant that the little road from Leyburn to Reeth was now no longer an ice rink, so we drove over the tops and, apparently, through some kind of shooting range.

Red flags were flying, and smoke was billowing presumably as some kind of warning to any half-witted hikers who might foolishly consider a wander across these moors today, so we stayed firmly on the road and headed for our destination.

The road was fun, twisting and turning this way and that, with the odd stomach-churning hillock threatening to remove one's stomach contents at any moment and completely without notice.

I had not had breakfast today, so I was not at risk, though there was always Rob, I chuckled. As his face turned a rather deep shade of red, however, I remembered that we were in my car, so I finally decided to use the middle pedal of the car, more commonly known as the brake, of course, and slowed down for the rest of the miles.

Once again, Belle had spent the entire journey snoring her head off on the back seat, though as soon as the car came to a halt on the village green in Reeth, she was immediately sat bolt upright, clearly eager to get out of the car as soon as that door opened.

We had the village more or less to ourselves today, with only a couple of fellow hikers visible who were clearly getting ready to move off. The shop was open but showed no signs of activity, and it was too early for the bus, so with not much to interest us here, we were soon kitted up and ready to go ourselves.

The sun was slowly rising from the eastern horizon, which today was hanging as it did above a cloudless sky of the deepest blue. Hopefully, this would remain the case for the full day, although we would, at some point, inevitably find ourselves walking straight into it, of course.

Today's route would take us out of Reeth and first to Grinton, a tiny village with little more than a church and a pub, although some would say what more does a village need? We would then head up onto the tops and follow a huge swirling arc around the unusually named Gibbon Hill to a crossroads of several paths.

A right turn would then lead us down into Castle Bolton, after which we would finally head west towards Aysgarth, where hopefully we would discover that Rob had remembered his car keys and had not left them in my car like he did once before, something which I will never let him forget, ever.

We followed the road down the hill, then, and round the bend, so to speak, back to the bridge that we had driven over on our way in. This is a rather nice bridge, it has to be said, and crosses a little stream called Arkle Beck in quite some style, what with its three impressive arches. It was designed and built by a man called John Carr, who was, by all accounts, one of the most prolific architects in the country during the 1700s.

He was very good at doing what he did, too, judging by this bridge, and although Carr won't necessarily be remembered for this alone, or for anything come to think of it, he did design some rather nice buildings in his time, including the magnificent Harewood House near Leeds as well as the beautiful Buxton Crescent in, well, Buxton, I imagine. The fact that he was a good architect is not merely my humble opinion, but it is a fact. He built another sixty bridges across Yorkshire, most of which are not only still standing but are in fantastic condition and form the backbone of the road system around here to this very day.

In fact, and I hadn't realized this until I did a fair bit of digging, we had already walked across a couple of his bridges back at Bainbridge, with more yet to come at Grinton and Aysgarth, so I guess he liked it around here. This is perhaps because he lived not far away, in York, where he somehow also found the time to be the Lord Mayor. A very busy man indeed.

We did pop across the road here for a momentary diversion. The Coast-to-Coast Path still follows the same route as the Herriot Way at this stage, and just next to the bridge, some enterprising soul has placed what looked like a tank on a car forecourt. We had stopped here on the cross-country route some years before for a photo opportunity, and we did exactly the same today. Taking a couple of silly photos of us up against the armoured car, which suggested we were perhaps being arrested, Rob then sent one to Chris, as he had been with us the last time we had been up here.

Silliness over, we carried on our way, following a hedged-in path next to the stream, where I let Belle off her lead for the first time today. She had been pulling and tugging as we left Reeth and clearly could not wait to be set free, and as soon as I did so, she was immediately off, enjoying herself once more.

Unfortunately, another dog walker appeared after just a minute, so her short-lived freedom was exactly that. I kept her on the lead after this as we would soon be at Grinton and back on the road, though I don't think she was very happy at this decision, to be honest, judging by the look she gave me.

The bridge at Grinton was just as impressive as the one at Reeth, though it was thankfully somewhat wider, and while we considered which way to go next, we hid in a recess to allow traffic to pass as this road was also much busier than the last, which was odd because it was the same road.

The map told us to head south over the bridge, which meant we would leave both the Coast-to-Coast Path and the River Swale behind once and for all now, both of which would head east from here while we went south.

We crossed the bridge into the village, with the impressive church, St Andrew's, to our immediate right. Dubbed The Cathedral of the Dales by many, it is clear to see why, so I asked Rob and Belle if they wanted to go and have a sniff around inside.

Unfortunately, a dog walker grabbed us momentarily and told us that the church would be locked and that dogs aren't allowed in either, and he also told me to pick up any poop, which I thought was a bit cheeky, to be honest. He said he wasn't local but was up here for the week and was having an awful time. He also told us it would rain later and that we would get wet through, something I found to be strange judging by the cloudless sky currently visible all around. I had soon slowly managed to edge away from him and fully planned to leave Rob to do the talking, as everything that came out of this guy's mouth was totally negative, and I could see the alarm on Rob's face when he realized I was trying to abandon him.

When we finally managed to sneak away, I mentioned to Rob that of all of the eight billion people on the planet, we had to meet him. Rob replied that some people are like slinkies. They are not good for much, but they put a smile on your face when you push them down the stairs. We moved on.

I'll be honest, it was a close thing between the pub and the church as they were opposite each other, and we almost succumbed to the pub in fact, but, being a bit of a geek, I explained to Rob that I was a little excited about something I expected to find in the church. Anyway, the pub was shut.

The door to the church was thankfully unlocked, so we ventured in and began our exploring. It's not mice we were looking for today, I told Belle, but it is a hagioscope. She looked at me as if she didn't understand, but then I guess she didn't.

A hagioscope is an architectural term for a squint, which is basically a hole cut through, or more accurately built into, a masonry wall that gives worshippers a view of the altar. They were sometimes used for lepers, who would be placed in a separate room to keep them away from the rest of the population, you see. I wondered if John Haygarth had taken inspiration from this hagioscope and its intention to keep the lepers from the healthy folk, as it is highly likely that he would have visited this church when he grew up in this area, and if you remember, he spent his entire career working on methods to prevent diseases spreading.

Anyway, not many churches have them, and often, those that did have them have filled them in at some point. I looked around for a while but found nothing, as did Rob and Belle until I realized I was looking in the wrong place. It turns out that the squint at Grinton is built into the exterior wall and was indeed designed to allow lepers to see into the church, though when I looked through it to the outside, all I could see was a tree.

Next to the squint are a couple of large signs telling the story of the church's bat colony, which is an unexpected bonus. I had to take my glasses off to read the sign, as I'm actually a bit short-sighted, and I often refer to myself as being as blind as a bat without them. Well, I've been wrong all my life, apparently, as the signs tell me that bats are not actually blind but just rely on echolocation when they are out hunting at night. In fact, bats probably have better eyesight than you or I, according to this sign anyway.

While we're on the subject of bats, it's commonly thought that they are the inspiration for all of the many vampire stories that are very popular nowadays, but this is simply not true. Bloodsucking bats were only discovered in the 16th century in South America, while stories of vampires go back to 12th century Europe, which begs the question of where the idea came from then?

The church has another oddity, something that used to be quite common but is now very rare, and that is a chained church bible. It's not because the people of Grinton are a bit light-fingered, although you never know, but it is, in fact, probably a relic from a bygone age. The bible dates from 1752, believe it or not, so I dared not touch it, as it was almost as old as Rob. It is believed to be here due to an edict issued by Henry VIII sometime after the reformation, which was basically his way of telling the Catholic church that he was the boss from now on and that Protestantism was the new black and they had better do as they were told. And as well they should have, because, during his thirty-six-year reign, old Henry had around 57,000 people variously hanged, beheaded or tortured to death, including, of course, one or two of his wives.

Lastly, there are many memorials in the church, but one sticks out like a sore thumb, as it relates to a family called the Swales, who can trace their family tree right back to the Battle of Hastings, apparently. My mind immediately wonders if this family is the origin for the name of the dale and with it the river, of course.

We ventured back outside, and I made a point of having a look through the hagioscope and was surprised to find that it offered a pretty good view of the altar. While it would certainly have given whoever was using it a rough idea of what was going on inside, I could not help but feel sorry for them. I mean, at some point in the past, real people would definitely have stood on this very spot and used this little window, and they would undoubtedly have been classed as outcasts.

I shuddered and moved on, catching Rob up, who was already at the gate and seemed to be wondering which direction we were headed in. I pointed him to the right, and while we walked, I told him about the mad dog of Grinton.

If you cast your mind back to when we passed Calvert Houses on the walk into Gunnerside, I had mentioned that a dog had been cornered and killed there following a rampage across Swaledale. Well, that rampage began here in Grinton, so it really did run amok across the whole of the dale.

The dog that caused so much trouble around here started off first of all by going berserk and attacking the cattle dogs of a man called John Metcalf. It then moved on to bite a young boy, who was the servant of the local landlady. Following this, it moved on to Reeth, where it savaged a dog owned by a Mr Bell who lived in the village, before it then dashed across the fields to Healaugh, where it mauled a spaniel.

Finally, and as we have already heard, just west of Ivelet at Calvert Houses, it was cornered and killed, but not before it left a trail of destruction that stretched from one end of the dale to another.

This wasn't the end of it, though. All of the animals that were bitten then also had to be destroyed, and yet more animals, which had subsequently been bitten by John Metcalf's dog back at Grinton, had to be killed too, as allowing them to live could see them also go on to develop rabies, and therefore spread the terror even further. I could not find out what had happened to the little boy, but I suspect the worst, as there is no cure for rabies nowadays, never mind in the 1800s.

We're very lucky today in that rabies is now more or less unknown in the United Kingdom, having been eradicated once and for all by 1922 in terrestrial animals, although bats occasionally continue to test positive, so don't get bitten by any whatever you do. I wish I had known that before I went into the church here, I thought.

If you do happen to get bitten by a rabid animal, by the way, then the first symptom might well be a bad mood, I kid you not. This will probably soon progress to flu-like symptoms, followed quickly by cerebral dysfunction, anxiety, confusion, agitation, and finally and perhaps quite happily after going through all of that, death. The only way to avoid the grim reaper is to seek medical assistance as soon as you have been bitten because once the virus has taken hold, it is already too late.

Having had enough of death, we moved on, heading out of the village, though Rob was keeping at least one eye on Belle just in case she started licking her lips and salivating or went into a bad mood. The village ended more or less straight away, and we found ourselves going up a very steep hill indeed, which at least served to warm us up a bit. I'm not saying it was steep, though I wished I had brought some crampons and ropes, but anyway, after passing through an impossibly narrow squeeze followed by several swing gates that separated each field, we found ourselves at a small road, but not, unfortunately, at the top of the hill.

The road took us higher, and on the left, we saw what looked like a small castle, though it was actually the Youth Hostel. Herriot stayed here with his son on their little walk, and it was a very nice building, so it was a shame we were not stopping there today.

Not surprisingly, it has not always been a Youth Hostel. It originally started out as a shooting lodge and actually has rather a lot of history. Originally built for a man called James Felton, it eventually came into the ownership of the Charlesworth family, which is when things got interesting. I always try to get my home town of Hull into my various walks and stories, so I am more than happy to tell you that the Charlesworths came from Hull, or at least I was happy until I found out about John Charlesworth, who actually turned out to be dishonourable, unscrupulous, deceitful, untrustworthy and shameful. In other words, he was a politician.

John became the Member of Parliament for Wakefield, and as he originally stood unopposed, he was elected without incident. He didn't do much for the town, it has to be said, and he only spoke in Parliament on three occasions throughout his first term, so he earned his money pretty easily when you think about it.

When the next election rolled around, a man called William Henry Leatham took one look at Charlesworth's easy job and decided that he wanted a piece of that. He was determined to get it, too, and pulled out all the stops during his campaign, beating Charlesworth by just three votes once the count was in.

Charlesworth cried foul and demanded not just a recount but a full-on investigation, accusing Leatham of employing such illicit tactics as bribery and intimidation, among others, though in retrospect, this was perhaps not Charlesworth's best move ever and was one that actually led to his own eventual downfall and also signified the beginning of an incredibly bad stretch of luck for him and his family, to put it mildly.

Following what was actually a surprisingly impartial and thorough investigation, the Committee on Elections concluded in late 1859 that Leatham had indeed conducted a thoroughly rotten campaign and had, in fact, spent £3,900 bribing various constituents and making promises of favourable treatment to those who voted for him.

All sounds good for Charlesworth, then, but unfortunately, the Committee also found that not only did John Charlesworth employ the exact same tactics, he actually spent more money bribing constituents than Leatham ever did, some £4,150. However, this was not all they uncovered as they also discovered that Charlesworth had himself employed some rather famous prize-fighters to beat a few people up, just in case anyone had the silly idea of taking a bribe from Leatham instead and voting for him.

It turns out that voters were more or less auctioned off to the highest bidder, and it became something of a scandal at the time, and this fiasco promptly ended Charlesworth's political career once and for all. However, no criminal charges were brought, which was perhaps not surprising, as Charlesworth was untouchable due to his lofty position within society.

Perhaps we should be thankful that we now live in an age where politicians respect the outcomes of elections, treat people with honesty and respect, and don't consider themselves above the law. Oh, wait a minute, we don't.

Anyway, going back to Grinton Lodge, you will see that it is perfectly adapted for wheelchair users if you ever happen to find yourself there. This isn't something that has been done recently either, but it was done way back in the 1800s, which is quite unusual, I am sure you will agree.

John Charlesworth had a son, you see, a man called Albany, who eventually inherited the lodge, and who had even worse luck than his father. At some point, Albany had a rather bad accident with a pheasant and ended up spending the rest of his life in a wheelchair. I'm not kidding, he was out hunting one day, and things went badly wrong, and although it was probably his shotgun or the horse he was on that did the actual damage, there was definitely a pheasant involved nonetheless, so we shall blame the bird.

Anyway, Albany had the lodge completely renovated and spent the rest of his life there. Later on, Albany himself had a son, also called Albany, although everyone called this one Barney, and it is Barney who next inherited the lodge, living there quite happily with his wife Diane and their son David.

You've probably guessed that this is not going to be a happy-ever-after type of story by now, and you are, of course, completely correct because the Second World War then blew up in all of their faces, shattering everyone's lives forever.

At the start of the war, Barney did the only thing he could, which was to join the army and head off to Europe to sort out Hitler. He wasn't actually fighting, of course, as he was rich, so instead, he was appointed to the position of aide-de-camp to Field Marshall Alan Brooke, who was basically the head of the British Army. An aide-de-camp, by the way, is simply a confidential assistant, so he would have been privy to all sorts of wartime secrets and would have known that the Field Marshall was very critical of Winston Churchill and didn't really like him all that much.

Being with people at such high levels of government office, Barney would also have known Churchill, so he presumably kept his mouth shut about all that he had heard, though much of it later came out anyway when Brooke published his memoirs after the war, in which he was openly critical of Churchill.

Anyway, in February of 1945, Barney found himself following his boss and Churchill to the Yalta Conference, where the Prime Minister would meet President Roosevelt and Joseph Stalin to carve up much of Europe and decide who was getting which countries once the fighting finally stopped, but this is where Barney's luck also ran out.

The plane he was on had been following a roundabout route in order to stay safe and had headed down to the Mediterranean before turning east towards Yalta. Unfortunately, on 1st February, it crashed near Pantelleria, a small island halfway between

Tunisia and Italy, and although a handful of people did survive, Barney was among those killed and was later buried on the island of Malta. This tragedy was mentioned by both the Field Marshall and the Prime Minister in their memoirs and diaries, and while Brooke described the incident as his greatest personal loss in the war, Churchill basically shrugged his shoulders and said that's life.

And in a final blow to the Charlesworth family, Barney's son David was killed in a road traffic accident in Palestine in 1946, just over a year after his father's death, and was buried in Haifa, Israel. Not surprisingly, perhaps, after the loss of her whole family, Diane felt she could no longer live in the lodge and immediately sold it, which is exactly when it became a Youth Hostel, of course.

As I looked at the Youth Hostel today, I imagined that most people who stay there have no idea of the history of the place or of the tragedy of the Charlesworth family, but then why would they? I imagine most old buildings would tell all sorts of tales if they could talk, and this is one of the things I enjoy most about getting out into the countryside, which is learning about new places and the people who lived there.

However, it was time to move on, and our path left the road opposite the hostel, taking us east and onto Harkerside Moor. There were no sheep around, which was good for Belle, as she was once again off her lead, and this was because the grazing of sheep has been increasingly discouraged up here, primarily so that the land can be managed more in favour of noisy things with feathers, which certain rich people can then shoot and eat.

Belle was more than a little scared when one of those noisy things with feathers flew out from beneath the heather, and she soon ran back to us in complete fear of something that was actually no bigger than a kitten. I think it was a grouse, but it was that quick, it was hard to tell for sure and was soon gone. You can come up here and shoot them if you want, either with a camera or a gun, if that is your thing, and you can also bag yourself other tasty treats such as snipe, pheasant and partridge, or even salmon and trout. I don't think you can actually shoot the fish, though, unless you really are using a camera.

We wandered on, with the path slowly taking a more uphill aspect, and across the valley to our left, we could see a small hut far off in the distance. I had heard there are several dotted around here, good for sheltering in if the weather takes a turn for the worse, and I had hoped to come across one to have a look, but this particular one was too far off the beaten track.

Rob and I chatted as we wandered along, enjoying the countryside all around us and feeling on top of the world. We could see for miles in all directions and decided that we had managed to pick an absolutely ideal day to do this walk, which led us to the odd question of where was everybody?

Whenever we are out walking, we usually bump into all sorts of people, but today we had only seen a couple, and one of them we had wished we hadn't. I wasn't complaining, of course. If it had been packed out here, it would have no doubt annoyed us, so I was enjoying the solitude of it all, and with nobody around, I knew that it was safe to let Belle run free.

I was a little concerned that she might chase a bird of one kind or another, but she seemed to be sticking to the path for the time being, and anyway, like I said, I think she was scared of them. I didn't think that any of these birds would be nesting yet, being the heart of winter as it was, although I was a little concerned about Belle running off and disappearing down a disused mine shaft or sinkhole, which were marked on the map I had and which were apparently all around us.

The path here was generally good and easy to follow, but it soon became quite steep once again. The ascent was short and sharp, however, and we were soon at the top of High Harker Hill, where we once again enjoyed stunning views in all directions.

Swaledale stood to our west, an amazing patchwork of fields

bounded by dry-stone walls, with many of them containing a barn, or as we had learned to call them last time, a cow house. Gunnerside was just about visible, with the moor rising steadily above and behind it, and in every other direction were unnamed moors, unnamed to us at least, of all shapes and sizes.

The one hill we could name was Gibbon Hill, which was the one we were currently following the contours of and which we would continue to do so for some hours yet. It dawned on me that as we rounded this hill, however, there would soon come the point where we would be walking directly into the sun, and every step took us closer to this eventuality.

I'm going to be a bit vague now, as I don't want to give away the exact location, but we soon stumbled on a small cabin which certainly managed to attract our interest. It didn't look new, but it was certainly not run-down, and as we got close, we realized it was not locked.

Rob tried the door, and it opened a fraction, although an old shoelace was all that was keeping it closed. Rob had gloves on, so I said I would untie it, although when I tried, I was surprised to find my fingers clumsy and unresponsive, as I had not realized they had become so cold.

I eventually managed to untie the door, and when we went in, we were met with an absolute jackpot of a hut. A table and chairs allowed people to sit, and at one end of the cabin was a rather nice wood stove along with a sizeable pile of logs. The roof looked solid enough, and if you happened to be passing by here on a bad weather day, I imagine you would be very happy indeed to stumble upon this hut. I could not see a sign that either allowed or forbade our use of the hut, and I had no idea who owned it, but the fact that it was left unlocked suggested that it was okay to come in and take shelter if needed.

Rob and I, along with Chris, had stayed in something similar a while back when we had walked the West Highland Way. This had been Rowchoish Bothy, on the bonny banks of Loch Lomond, and we had enjoyed it immensely, despite or perhaps because of the fact that we were sharing with complete strangers.

The bothy in Scotland had been easy to find, being well-known and part of a network of bothies run by a professional association of like-minded people. However, bothies in England are as rare as the proverbial, so to speak, and you will not find one by scouring the internet or reading books. You will have to get out there and walk some miles, and if you do happen to come across one, then you should consider yourself very lucky indeed.

Don't shout about them, though, and while it's alright to share knowledge with responsible people, don't give them exact directions but let them make the discovery themselves. That way, they are worthy.

Moving on from our undisclosed location, we continued on our way, and as mentioned not long ago, we soon found ourselves heading straight for the sun. I have those glasses that turn into sunglasses, but even when they had gone as dark as they were ever going to get, I still felt as if I was being blinded.

I tried walking along while looking at the floor, but after almost falling into a ravine, I once again raised my head, squinting as I struggled to see. Eventually, I figured out that by walking in the shadow of the giant in front of me, I would at least be able to see whichever bank I might happen to fall down.

Isolated pockets of snow dotted the shaded side of the track, which was to my right, and after a long and featureless stretch of path, things suddenly became a lot more interesting. The route descended into a small valley, twisting left and right and dropping down a somewhat steep and gravelly track, and it was as I was taking my camera out of my pocket to take a picture of this pretty scene that my right foot slipped on the stony gravel.

My knee collapsed towards the ground at the same time as I dropped my camera, and I watched it in slow motion on its free-fall to what looked like certain death. My ankle twisted further, and I felt pain shoot rapidly up my leg, which was all a problem, of course, but there was an even bigger problem. Rob and Belle had stopped dead in their tracks at the sudden commotion from behind and were now both splitting their sides in uncontrollable laughter.

And if you think dogs can't laugh, then you are wrong, my friend, because one was laughing at me right now. I managed to drag myself up before Rob could get an incriminating photo that would have inevitably done the rounds, and I completely ignored his shouts of don't move.

My knee felt okay, but my ankle was definitely not, but just like last time, I decided to walk it off as if I stood still to rest it, I was pretty sure it would start to hurt more and begin to stiffen. After a hundred yards of this, I began to wonder if I had made a mistake, as the pain seemed to have increased, especially on the uphill, but I carried on regardless, although I felt that I had definitely slowed down a little. As for my camera, well, that was destroyed.

Luckily, the twisting and turning of the path regularly eased the pain, and as a double bonus, we were now heading downhill.

The path straightened out a little and levelled off, and at the same time, it became smoother and easier to walk on. A layer of soft sand had replaced loose stones, and while I figured that this was probably a much safer walking surface, it was nonetheless a little bit too late.

There was probably only a mile or so to go until our scheduled lunch stop, and in that mile, I did feel the pain lessen a little, which reassured me that I had done the right thing by not stopping.

Unfortunately, the path was still quite featureless at this stage, and although we appeared to be dropping down into a shallow valley, there was not a lot to see that would have given you any indication of where you were.

However, after a few hundred yards more and after rounding

a bluff to our left, we saw our intended target far off in the distance. We now knew that it would only be a few moments more before we could have our lunch, and I think Belle got a sense of that too, especially when I used certain words such as dinner and biscuit, which certainly seemed to make her ears prick up.

It was more or less at lunchtime, then, that we arrived at Dent House for our lunch. The house, if you can call it that, sits at a crossroads, and from here, we would be heading south, but not before having our food.

I fed Belle first and tried to encourage her to have a drink of water, but she wasn't interested in it and was merely waiting for the main course. I dug her food from the bottom of my rucksack, and within mere seconds she was tucking into her meaty treat.

I had just sat down to eat my own when I noticed her staring at me out of the corner of my eye. I was only onto the second bite of my sandwich, but somehow Belle had eaten her whole dinner and was now eyeing up my food as well. I turned away from her, but she simply moved around, and those big sad doggy eyes finally made me succumb to her plight, and she ultimately ended up eating my sausage roll. After that, I just ignored her.

Rob pulled a flask out of his bag and poured us both a coffee, which was an unexpected treat, and he also produced a chocolate bar, which disappeared out of his hand faster than you can say, overweight middle-aged chubby bloke. Still, it tasted lovely.

I had brought my drone along today, and after eating every scrap of food in my bag, I flew it briefly, just to get a photo or two of where we were, and after no more than twenty minutes, we were ready to go again.

There was a short climb up the hill, over the other side of which was Castle Bolton, or was it Bolton Castle? In truth, both were over there, but anyway, as we walked, we both agreed that we should head back up here later in the year to stay in one of those mountain huts for a night. What could be better than good company, a bit of firewood and a wee dram, we figured?

The path was once again well-defined and easy to follow, yet was still devoid of walkers, despite the continued good weather. The sun was now to our right, which was good, although it was starting to drop down a little, which was bad, and as we topped the brow of the hill, we caught our first glimpse of Bolton Castle.

From behind us, we heard a bark, which was odd, as Belle was in front of us, apparently trying to jam her head permanently into a rabbit burrow, and as we turned, we saw the source of the noise. A small red-setter was bounding towards us with his owner running frantically behind, clearly trying to catch up with his escaped dog, though by the looks of it, he never stood a chance.

The dog sniffed Belle, and with her hair now standing on end, she seemed perfectly still and completely unsure of what to do. After a split-second of wondering which dog would kill the other, the red-setter barked and ran off, clearly hoping that Belle would chase after him, but she just returned to her rabbit hole instead and ate some droppings.

The man was called Rich, though he didn't look it, although he was very nice and chatty and was much more pleasant than the last person we had met. He was staying up here because his wife was planning some kind of suicidal long-distance run, he said, but scoffed at the idea when I asked him if he was also joining in such masochistic shenanigans. He said that he'd walk Fluffy instead, and I presumed Fluffy to be the cute little furball that was currently attempting to pluck and disembowel a pheasant in the bushes to our right. He shouldn't be hungry, really, said Rich, as he had already had a rabbit for breakfast, and I'm not sure if he was kidding or if he was serious.

It didn't matter anyway, as, at that moment, I tripped up once again and went head-first into the muddy ground beneath me. I was pretty impressed with myself, however, when I rebounded straight back up in a manner that reminded me of a spring, and I was soon back upright and professing that I was okay and that

I had not hurt myself, even though I was covered in mud from head to foot.

We walked with Rich to the outskirts of the village, which is Castle Bolton, I remembered, and while he wandered off with his murderous pet, we stopped for a minute, not so much for a rest, but mainly to fly the drone and get a photo of the castle from the air.

The impressive hulk of Bolton Castle lay before us, in the heart of the village that almost but not quite bears its name, the perhaps dyslexic Castle Bolton. This is your classic British Castle, at least from the outside, and is probably what most of us would draw if we were asked to produce a picture of something like this.

Originally built in the 1300s by a man called Richard Scrope, pronounced scroop, by the way, who went on to become the 1st Baron of Bolton, the castle had seen some interesting years, and has, as we briefly heard earlier, variously acted as a prison to none other than Mary Queen of Scots and was almost destroyed when the 8th Baron, John Scrope, chose the wrong side in a dispute with King Henry VIII, which was clearly never a good idea.

The story of Mary Queen of Scots is perhaps the most interesting part of the castle's history, though. After being defeated at the Battle of Langside up in Scotland in 1568, Mary was caught and initially imprisoned at Carlisle Castle under the watchful eye of Henry Scrope, the 9th Baron. Carlisle was not exactly suitable when it came to imprisoning former queens, though, so Henry brought Mary to his ancestral home here in the dales.

It should probably be mentioned, however, that imprisonment in the case of Mary Queen of Scots did not exactly mean that they locked her in a cell and threw away the key, and in fact, this is probably as far from the truth as you could get.

Mary, you see, was imprisoned here with around fifty of her staff to support her every need. In fact, she had so many staff that they could not all be accommodated in the castle, so it was at this time when several of the houses in the village were built purely to house Mary's entourage. This entourage included, among many others, three people to constantly clean her clothes, someone to read to her, a personal surgeon, four grooms, and quite mysteriously, two 'others'.

She was put up in the Baron's own personal chambers, probably in the southwest tower, which was kitted out with carpets, rugs, tapestries and furniture which had been 'borrowed' from nearby castles and fine houses. Indeed, Mary's own cousin, English Queen Elizabeth I, who was in fact directly responsible for Mary's imprisonment, even saw fit to lend her a kettle.

Furthermore, Mary was even allowed out of the castle on a regular basis. She particularly enjoyed riding and hunting in the beautiful countryside that surrounds the castle more or less whenever she wanted to but was accompanied by guards at all times. She spent much of the rest of her time getting her hair done, seriously, so once again, imprisonment in this sense does not quite convey her actual experience.

Alas, all of this was only temporary, and Mary spent just six months or so here, from July 1568 to January 1569, when she was trundled off to Tutbury Castle, which is where she spent much of the rest of her life until her head was finally removed from the rest of her in 1587. It actually took two blows to fully detach her noggin, which sounds barbaric, but she could perhaps consider herself lucky, as other similar executions are known to have gone disastrously wrong. For instance, when Margaret Pole, the Countess of Salisbury, was executed, it took the blundering axeman 11 attempts before he finally managed to completely disengage her coconut.

Anyway, when the executioner held up Mary's head to show everyone that she was definitely, absolutely, positively dead, as per the custom of the time, which was in fact perhaps a somewhat pointless custom bearing in mind her recently removed bonce, it turned out that he was merely holding her wig. Her actual head had fallen to the floor and had even bounced once or twice, I kid you not. At the same time, a small dog is then said to have emerged from hiding in among her many skirts, which proceeded to run around wailing loudly while rolling in the understandably large pool of sticky red stuff. You cannot make this stuff up, and I really do wonder why they don't teach us these things at school, as it would make it all so much more interesting.

Not surprisingly, this castle is said to be haunted by the restless spirit of Mary. Most recently, she is supposed to have been seen enjoying one of her many shady walks around the gardens, which does not mean that her walks were in any way nefarious, of course, just that she walked under the trees to keep out of the sun. Separately, another sighting has her sitting in a window dressed in her finest garbs, gazing longingly at the outside world, probably wondering why she has a headache.

But what about life in the castle for everyone else? Well, although it looks to be a grand and stately place to live, the sad truth is that it would not have been all that comfortable. For a start, other than going to church, hunting, and torturing your enemies, there would not, in fact, have been a great deal to do unless you count the bath you might have had every three months or so if you were lucky.

This brings us to the smell. Anyone living within the castle would have shared the space with dozens of other people and animals, which would obviously soon create a somewhat spicy atmosphere, to say the least. There was no running water, either, so there would be no way to flush the toilets, and in the sense that we understand toilets, they did not exist anyway. A hole in a piece of wood would see you drop your dumplings into a communal cesspit of horrors, which hopefully some unlucky bugger would empty every now and then to stop it building up and giving everyone dysentery, or worse, cholera.

On top of this, the castle would probably be full of rats. Come to think of it, it would definitely be full of rats, and we should remember that they have carried many great plagues over the last few centuries. It's probably a good job then that most people were half-drunk most of the time as it was safer to drink alcohol of almost any kind than it was to drink the water. Not exactly a rosy picture of the good old days, is it?

As for the castle itself, it is certainly an incredibly beautiful building without any doubt whatsoever. When it was built, it offered large and comfortable rooms that were quite frankly ahead of their time. They offered privacy to some of the occupants, which was almost unheard of at the time, but only to a select few, while everyone else had to share with the rats.

The staircase is interesting, too. Most staircases spiral clockwise to enable swordsmen to swing a sword and kill bad guys, presuming the swordsmen are right-handed, of course. However, at Bolton Castle, the main staircase spirals anti-clockwise, so perhaps the Barons were left-handed?

The stairs also had another oddity – trip steps were built into them, which were basically steps cut to unequal sizes specifically designed to trip people up in the darkness of the night, which sounds like a good idea until we remember that everyone was drunk most of the time. Regardless, it might be fun to get some of these installed at home, I mentioned to Belle. She does not say no, so I presume she is in full agreement.

If you do visit the place and manage to survive the steps, then you will see a large bed in what was Mary's room, though it is neither original nor was it there at the time of her little holiday. The bed arrived later and was given to the Baron because the original owners were convinced it was haunted. Despite a couple of exorcisms, those attempting to sleep in the bed continued to have nightmares and hallucinations, and it is said that no one has managed a full night in it yet.

If you look at the castle from the outside, it is hard to miss the fact that parts of it are what can only be described as missing. This is because it finally succumbed to some serious damage during the Civil War. The Baron at the time, John Scrope, who was merely a teenager, picked the wrong side, something which perhaps runs in the family, and backed the Royalist forces. When the Royalists ultimately lost the war, and John and his armies finally surrendered after being besieged for quite some time and having eaten all of their own horses just to stay alive, Parliament decided to slight the castle, which meant they blew quite a bit of it to pieces, but luckily for us, just enough of it was left intact, which makes it a great place to come for a picnic.

Before we leave the Scrope family for the last time, we need to go back to the 1st Baron for a minute, who was, of course, Richard le Scrope. I have already said that I always try to shoe-horn my home city of Hull into my books, and in this case, I can rightfully do so, as Richard married a girl called Blanche de la Pole, who was the daughter of William de la Pole, a wealthy merchant from Hull who became so rich, he made a living by lending money to the king.

Anyway, Richard was a bit of a character and was a highly regarded knight of the realm under both Richard II and then Henry IV. Unfortunately, he also managed to really annoy both of these kings, with Richard finally removing Scrope from office. Unfortunately, the new king, Henry IV, removed something much more serious, the head of Scrope's second-born son, William. He then had the head transported to London in a white basket and displayed for all to see on London Bridge. This was a not-so-subtle warning to all others to think very carefully when considering their monarch.

Somehow or other, Richard le Scrope managed to survive all of these antics, and this is possibly because it is said that he was, in fact, the truly perfect gentle knight described by none other than famous English scribe Geoffrey Chaucer in his most famous work, *The Canterbury Tales*, so there you go. His house is nice, too, but then they do say that an Englishman's home is his castle, which is quite literally true in this case. And when Richard did finally shuffle off this mortal coil, he left lots of money in his will, even going so far as leaving 13 shillings and 4 pence to every single last resident of Richmondshire.

Anyway, although castles are all very interesting, it was definitely time to move on, and there was a waterfall nearby that I had hoped we could visit. Nelly Force is just a quarter of a mile to the east of the village, halfway towards Redmire. However, Belle was looking at me in a way that suggested she wasn't bothered about going to visit it, and Rob was already heading in the opposite direction, so I took that as a no and followed him.

We headed south then, out of the village and down the hill, but stopped several times to look back at the impressive castle, which had the added benefit of being bathed in brilliant sunlight today. What I could not see was the impressive maze within the grounds of the castle, which I only noticed later on when I looked at the photos I had taken with the drone, but anyway, we didn't need a maze as we could usually manage to get lost without one.

As I turned and walked away, I remembered that it was at Bolton Castle that James Herriot proposed to Helen in the original television series, and if the place looks familiar to you, it may be because it was also one of the filming locations for the classic movie Ivanhoe starring Elizabeth Taylor.

The road-walking only lasted for a hundred yards or so, and we soon turned down a tiny overgrown lane that was incredibly narrow but quite pleasant. Belle was off her lead again, busy enjoying all of the strange smells, and the tiny track soon led us across the route of the old Wensleydale Railway. To the east, the trackbed looked in excellent condition, as did a bridge in the distance, and it didn't look like it would be a very difficult job to relay the lines and get the trains moving, but to the west, it was a different story. Tall bushes and saplings completely blocked the way, and this seemed to be the case for as far as we could see, which would obviously all have to be cleared before even anything small could run that way, never mind a great big steam engine.

We crossed a moderately busy road and headed for a path that took us to Thoresby Lane. Sheep dotted the fields initially, but when we found ourselves back onto a narrow lane, Belle was once again set free.

It's perhaps ironic that this stretch of the path seemed to be the muddiest we had encountered all day, and I laughed as Rob slid this way and that, and even Belle nearly went tumbling over. My smile was wiped from my face, though, when I too joined in the fun, and I found myself edging carefully along the sides of the path in a vain attempt to avoid the worst of the mud.

Belle wasn't bothered about the mess and just ploughed on through it, and I think she might even have been deliberately targeting the deepest puddles and the sloppiest bits. I chuckled as I realized we were heading to Rob's car and not mine, which would, of course, mean that by the time we had driven back to my car, Belle would have wiped most of her mud onto the seats in his. Not wanting this to come as a nasty surprise to him, I then made sure he knew how filthy my little four-legged friend was, but unfortunately, he didn't take the bait.

Due to the time of day, we now found ourselves walking straight into the low sun, which meant we could barely see anything in front of us. This is a problem normally, but doubly so today, given the treacherous state of the path we were on. In fact, come to think of it, it was a bit cheeky to call it a path at all, and it certainly was not like any lane I had been down before either.

Earlier in the day, I had suggested we take a short detour to Carperby, but this would add a mile or two onto our journey, so after a quick chat, I came up with a little plan. I suggested to Rob and Belle that once we were back at the car, we could instead drive to Carperby and perhaps pop into the pub, obviously in the spirit of supporting local businesses once again, of course. Well, you may be surprised to learn that Rob fully supported this plan, and I think Belle did too, as she never said anything to suggest otherwise.

For now, though, we carried on. Progress was slow, but a sign soon told us that we only had a couple of miles to go before we would arrive at Aysgarth, and as it was still pretty early, this meant that we would finish this walk while it was still light. I was a bit gutted at this, as my son had bought me one of those military-style torches that are good for illuminating entire football fields or for dazzling muggers, but alas, I would not be using mine today unless someone decided to rob me over the next couple of miles, of course.

We passed Hollins House, which I presumed to be a farm, and just after doing so, we heard the loud thunder of approaching aircraft. We couldn't see anything, but these things, whatever they were, were clearly low and fast, and with that, two military planes suddenly appeared just above the treetops and passed right overhead. We stopped walking and gazed upwards like two over-excited little boys. The pilots were clearly visible, and it was nice to spend a minute watching them fly down the whole of the valley, slowly banking to the right until they disappeared out of sight behind some trees as quickly as they had appeared. Belle, on the other hand, had sat down and appeared to be scratching her fleas.

Excitement over, we moved on, passing through a couple of nice-looking meadows, one of which was full of black calves. I had already put Belle back on her lead, but I could not see any signs of their mothers, and one thing I am wary of when out with Belle is that cows don't always like dogs, especially when their calves are around.

Rob was ahead of me anyway, and I told him that if there was any sign of trouble, I would let Belle go as she would have a better chance of getting away from any crazy bovine if she wasn't hamstrung by a chubby old man. Luckily, these calves were out on their own, so nothing happened, but you never know.

The path led us into some woods, and we could hear the sound of water getting louder and louder, which could only mean one thing. We were very close to Aysgarth Falls, which also meant we were very close to the finish.

Rob said he did not feel like he had walked all that far today and that he could easily go on, but let's just say I did not share this sentiment, and I was more than ready to stop walking. I didn't want to add any miles onto this walk, but the waterfalls proved to have quite a strong attraction, so we did go down some steps to look at where Robin Hood had smacked Little John in the you-know-whats. While we were down there, we briefly discussed which walk might be next, but neither of us could come up with anything.

There must have been a fair bit of rain over the last few days, as the falls were in good order today. I had last been here some years before at the height of summer, and it had been possible to wade out into the water and stand in the spot where they had fought. I had suggested to Rob that we do exactly that, and despite his name, Rob would have to be Little John, and I would be Robin Hood. We could use his hiking poles as swords to re-enact the scene, I told him, but for some reason, he had not been too keen at the prospect of being hit hard with a stick, in the crown jewels or anywhere else for that matter, he had said. Regardless, this would be impossible today, as anyone who attempted to stand in the river would no doubt be immediately washed to a splashy and probably quite swift demise.

With a photo or two in the bag, we moved on through the woods, coming out at the road into Aysgarth. We followed this over yet another one of John Carr's fabulous bridges, which really was rather splendid, and then the road led us up a hill and into the village itself, but not before we stopped to take yet another photograph of even more waterfalls, this time the Upper Falls which were on our right as we crossed the bridge.

Belle annoyed me here because she was pulling on her lead

constantly, and it took me a moment to figure out why. The road twisted sharply to the left up the hill, and she had lost sight of Rob, so she was craning her neck and trying to see around the corner to find out where he was. I reminded her that she was, in fact, my dog, but she was having none of it and simply wanted to get back to him.

Passing the church, I remembered that this is where James Herriot's car had famously lost its brakes and slid dangerously backwards down this very hill, stopping only when it hit a low stone wall. Had it not stopped, he could have died here, which reminded me of our own backward adventure on the frozen roads that had dogged our last trip up here.

At the top of the hill, we passed the old Youth Hostel, and while I know it is definitely no longer functioning as a hostel, I have no idea what it currently is. I found a phone number for the place and tried to ring them, but the line proved to be dead, and on passing the building, which is just on the corner of the main road opposite the Aysgarth Falls Hotel, it looked just like a house. Feeling a bit cheeky, I knocked on the door, but unfortunately, nobody answered, so it will have to remain a mystery, at least for now.

Anyway, this is where Herriot stayed on the first night of his walk, which had been a Friday night, in case you are wondering. He initially had at least a little apprehension about staying under a tiled roof rather than camping, describing such behaviour as *a little effete*, but he allowed himself to be persuaded nonetheless, presumably by his son, and here they stayed. I don't blame them one bit, either. I had wild camped, so to speak, on many long-distance walks, and although we had never actually died, there have been what we can only call incidents.

In the bothy in Scotland, we had nearly smoked ourselves like kippers, probably due to an unswept chimney, while simultaneously sharing the place with a rather scary complete stranger-cum-psychopath. On the Cleveland Way, Storm Frances had swept in, promptly putting an end to any silly ideas we may have had about sleeping under canvas, and on the Yorkshire Three Peaks, we had been eaten alive by the worst midge problem that Rob and I can ever recall encountering. So yes, I can fully understand why he chose to use hostels.

It was but a short walk to the centre of Aysgarth, marked by the war memorial where we had started, and I could feel Belle speed up slightly as we had approached the car. She knew the end was nigh, so to speak, and as soon as the car door was opened, she jumped straight in and made herself comfortable on the back seat, curling up into a little ball and spreading the finest Yorkshire mud deep into the velour. Good dog, I thought.

After a quick change into less-muddy footwear, we did exactly what we said we would do and drove to Carperby, fully intending to support the local economy.

The Wheatsheaf Inn has an interesting James Herriot connection and is well worth a visit, as this is where he spent his real-life honeymoon in 1941. Strangely enough, just a few weeks after his celebrity visit, Hollywood star Greta Garbo also stayed here. She had been entertaining troops at the nearby army base in Catterick.

Anyway, inside the pub, a letter on display sent by Herriott to his parents describes his wedding to Joan Danbury, who became Helen Herriot in his books. He describes how the vicar asked him if he would take Joan as his lawful wedded husband, which is, of course, strange and hopefully a mere slip of the tongue, but what is stranger still is that this suggests his parents were not at his wedding.

The answer to this question is actually rather sad. His parents never approved of the marriage but instead hoped he would marry into high society. Sadly, his mother never accepted him for what he was, which is actually quite ironic, as later on, of course, he became rich and famous beyond anything anyone would or could have hoped or expected, particularly for a humble vet. All of this was solely down to his mother's delusions of grandeur, with her having worked as a dressmaker, work which brought her into contact with the upper class. Hence, she refused to come to the wedding, and his father also stayed away in solidarity, something which affected Herriot greatly in his later years.

He first met Helen, of course, when he attended her farm to fix a broken leg on a calf. She then took her dog, which had suffered a dislocated hip, to his surgery, which begs the question of what exactly was she doing to these animals just so she could get a date with the local vet? I'm sure she wasn't, of course, nudge nudge, wink wink.

For me, Lynda Bellingham became the face of Joan Danbury or Helen Herriot, as she was the most memorable actress, in my mind anyway, who played her in the original series. Of course, for the first couple of seasons, her part was played by Carol Drinkwater, but I guess I am just too young to remember her as clearly.

Anyway, the story of how they met is not told entirely accurately in the television series. In real life, Helen was not a farmer's daughter at all but worked as a secretary in Thirsk, and Alf Wight met her at a dance, although she is said to have caused something of a stir in the town when she became the first woman there to wear pants, something that seems totally ridiculous nowadays, of course.

As for other notable characters from the original series, the one that stands out for me was Peter Davison, who played Tristan Farnon, who, let's just say, was the interesting brother of Siegfried and who, if you remember, we came across at the Kings Arms back in Askrigg. Of course, Davison became much better known when he scooped the part of Doctor Who for much of the 1980s, and here's an interesting fact, did you know that David Tennant, who of course went on to become rather a successful Doctor Who himself, is actually married to Peter Davison's daughter? Neither did I.

I will have to take a minute now, as all of these names are beginning to confuse me. For instance, on top of James Herriot really being Alf Wight, and Lynda Bellingham playing the part of Helen Alderson who became Helen Herriot who is really Joan Danbury, I have just found out that Peter Davison is really called David Moffet and David Tennant is really called David McDonald. My, oh my.

On top of that, different actors have variously played all of these people, either in the original film or the first television series in 1978 and in the new television series that began in 2020. I thought my head was going to explode, being of very little brain as I am.

As we went into the pub to officially finish this walk and discuss where we would go next, we both noticed a sign on the wall that said the Wheatsheaf Inn was, in fact, pub number eighteen along *The Inn Way*, another long-distance footpath in the dales, and as I looked at Rob and he looked at me, I think I can confidently say that we both knew exactly which walk would be next after all.

OVER THE TOPS

Keld to Reeth (Again)

Many people have told me that there is no day five on the Herriot Way, but they are wrong, as here we were, on the fifth day of this walk, defying the known laws of physics, apparently. Anyway, we had chosen to repeat the route from Keld to Reeth, this time via the high route, and we were once again going to walk from west to east. We could, in retrospect, have simply turned around when we had finished the low route at Reeth and taken the high route back to Keld, finishing there. Indeed, for reasons of simplicity, that would make sense. You would not, for instance, have to worry about transport and logistics and could simply make Keld our ultimate finish point, but there would be one tiny flaw if you chose to do so. That flaw would be death.

I'm serious. For a start, you would be walking directly into the weather and in the middle of winter, which would mean freezing to death. But even this death would not be simple. First of all, your nose would freeze, resulting in frostbite, but you would then hear a strangely satisfying thud as it hit the ground shortly after it fell off. Your ears would be next, after which you would hear nothing, and then, one by one, all of your bodily extremities would slowly disappear, one by one, until you had none left.

Furthermore, at any time of the day other than midnight or dawn, you would also find yourself walking directly into the sun, and given the treacherous nature of the high route, you would almost definitely take a step forward at some point, only to find the ground curiously missing. You would then freefall, somewhat lemming-like, to a squishy death on the rocks below, where some poor cub scouts would inevitably be traumatized for life when they found your mushed up remains sometime in late spring when your stiff corpse would finally thaw out.

So, bearing this in mind, we had chosen to walk west to east. Walk east to west at your peril, my friend.

Actually, the real reason we were walking in this direction was because that way, the wind is usually behind you, and that really is true.

Anyway, the day started out much as the others had, although in this case, somewhat earlier. I had offered to pick Rob up at 6am and thus set my alarm for 5am. When it went off, I quite surprised myself by jumping spritefully out of bed and getting dressed at a speed and in a manner that is, quite frankly, not my usual self. Normally, my day starts out at a much more relaxed pace, which I can perhaps demonstrate by asking you to think of the start of a race, in this case, one involving several Giant African Land Snails that have all just been dosed up with sleeping tablets.

How surprised was I then, when I came downstairs, made a cup of coffee, and went to watch the news. It wasn't so much the news itself that was surprising, but it was *which* news I was watching that got me. I had rewound to the beginning of the programme, but only by a couple of minutes, and I almost spat my drink out when I heard the presenter wish me a very good morning and welcome me to the four o'clock news.

Four o'clock? I can only assume I had knocked the clock somehow when I set it the night before, and I immediately felt as if I had been robbed of an hour's sleep, one that I would never get back, ever. And thinking about it, I should have suspected something was off when I walked past Belle's bed, when she merely raised her head, gave me a rather surprised but definitely sleepy look, and then went straight back to sleep.

Anyway, the day only got worse after that. After I finally dragged Belle out of her bed, funnily enough at the correct hour of 5 am, and after bribing her with some rather nice biscuits and a cup of tea, I decided to get the car off the drive. Unfortunately, the dog wasn't the only thing that was reluctant to move, and as I turned the key in the ignition, I heard the slow-motion turn of a starter motor, followed by some strange but seemingly pointless clicks. We were going nowhere in my car.

To cut a long story short, it was some time after 6 am when Rob picked me up, and with Belle soon asleep on the back seat, we were finally off.

While winter certainly wasn't over by any stretch of the imagination, the days were beginning to get just a little longer, which meant that dawn broke long before we arrived in Reeth. This gave us the chance to have a bit of a better look at the countryside as we made our way across the north of England, and it certainly wasn't disappointing.

A brilliant blue sky greeted us once again, and as we drove over the tops and headed downhill into Reeth, Rob did an absolutely fantastic job of dodging various suicidal rabbits and pheasants and, at one point, a rather stubborn sheep. The sheep was the closest call, as it jumped alarmingly into the road as we rounded a bend, and it was almost as if it wanted to die. Somehow, however, the expected collision never occurred, although I am sure all of those involved required new underwear soon after, including the sheep.

We parked in our usual spot, just opposite the shop, and as we were a bit early, we stayed in the car until the bus was due. We were catching the exact same one at the exact same time, so just before it was due, we changed into our walking shoes, put on our many layers, and ventured outside into the frozen north once again.

A bitter wind blew from the west, so I huddled next to a large van, and although I encouraged Belle to do the same, she was too busy sniffing the floor looking for snacks. Rob popped into the shop to buy some sweets, which I thought was tempting fate, as I had half-expected the bus to turn up as soon as he had disappeared.

However, it did not, and it had still not arrived after he had come back out. Glancing at my watch, the bus was now several minutes overdue, and even though we had caught this exact same bus on our last visit, I began to doubt myself and asked myself all sorts of questions.

Had the bus company cunningly changed their timetable and failed to inform us? Was my watch as wrong as my alarm clock had been? And do fish get thirsty?

Okay, maybe not the last one, although it is certainly an interesting question, but anyway, Rob then shouted that the bus was coming.

Only it wasn't, but what did turn up was a supermarket delivery truck, which, while being great for whoever had ordered milk and eggs just in time for breakfast, was absolutely no use to us.

A minute later, though, we were finally put out of our misery when the Little White Bus trundled up the road and came to a halt just a few feet in front of us.

Belle must have known we were getting on as she immediately pushed her way past the both of us and was clearly eager to embark. As the door slid open, though, she had second thoughts, and I wondered if she had suddenly remembered that she didn't like buses after all.

Rob was on first, however, and paid for us all, and when Belle finally jumped up those steps, she was soon in her favourite position, which was as far forward on the bus as possible.

We were the only passengers, and as we moved off, we soon struck up a conversation with the driver. He was called Andy, he said, and was originally from Bristol but had settled up here some years before. After a quick interrogation, which included asking him if he was Banksy, we concluded that he wasn't, though he was still very interesting to talk to. He told us about the villages along the way and about the company behind the Little White Bus, and he, too, had a great love of hiking and rambling. We told him about our little walk along the Herriot Way, and he told us about his recent walk along the Dales Way, which incidentally we made a mental note of, as this was a most interesting sounding walk if ever there was one.

The bus followed the same route as last time, although the obvious difference today was that we went as far as Keld and passed through Gunnerside, Muker and Thwaite without picking up any further passengers. Andy confirmed that we had been pronouncing Muker correctly, and as we pulled up into Keld, he told us to make sure we stopped in the self-service café, which we assured him we would.

As bus drivers go, he was probably one of the friendliest I had ever met, and he clearly loved his job, so we were quite disappointed when he drove off, as we could probably have spent all day talking to him about this and that.

Anyway, we had a walk to do and limited time to do it, but regardless of that, we took Andy's advice and popped into the café.

We all went in this time, as Belle was still spotlessly clean, having only been in a car or on a bus so far, and not in a field full of the finest sheep droppings or cowpats, like she had last time.

There was a fire on inside today, so after dropping our bags, I put the kettle on while Rob went to find a toilet in the village, and Belle just sniffed everything. And when I say everything, I mean everything. She ducked under the table, stuck her head above it to see what was up there, went up some stairs in a corner, and almost burnt her nose on the fire, though luckily it was behind a fireguard.

While I made us a coffee, and when I say us, I mean Rob and myself, as it would be silly to make Belle a coffee as everyone knows she only drinks tea, I found some dog biscuits, so I gave a couple to my faithful dog.

Fresh cakes and buns dotted the worktops, which all looked as nice as each other, but when Rob returned, we both decided on chocolate tiffin, and I must say that we made the right choice. Gulping down our coffee, which was too hot, Belle sniffed at our feet for any dropped crumbs and almost had a heart attack when the door swung open.

A man came in, smartly dressed and with grey hair, and he looked as surprised to see us as we were to see him. Rob asked him if he was walking today, but he said he was local and was working, not walking.

We soon struck up a conversation, and he explained that this café was only open out of season when the campsite was closed. He also told us a couple of interesting things about the building. The most interesting one was that a stream ran beneath it, which explained the holes in the floor, he added. To be honest, I had not noticed any holes in the floor, but sure enough, when I looked, there were a series of vents cut into the floor near the door, and he said these were there to stop damp collecting beneath our feet.

He didn't stay too long, and as soon as he shut the door behind him, I was on the floor and peering through the holes but could see nothing. Similarly, when I put my ear on the floor, I could not hear anything either. Standing up and dusting myself off, I concluded that he had been winding us up and that on a security camera feed somewhere, a couple of oldies were laughing their heads off at the chubby bloke on the floor and chalking another mark on their scoreboard.

It was time for us to make a move anyway, and while Rob did the washing up, I signed the visitors' book and particularly thanked them for the doggy biscuits, which had been a nice touch, and I am sure Belle would agree. In fact, I wrote that Belle had said thank you for the biscuits, which was a lie, as what she actually said was *woof*.

We moved out of the village to the east, following the same track we had for the low route last time, but turned north to cross the River Swale after a couple of hundred yards. This track led us steeply down, and we got talking about the dangers of walking alone.

Don't get me wrong. There are not too many dangers in walking alone, and I love my own company, up to a point anyway, but there are instances when it can come in handy to have someone with you.

For instance, on the last section, as we walked into Aysgarth, I had sent Rob ahead of me as a decoy for the calves, although I had not stated that this had been the mission at the time. Similarly, while on the Coast-to-Coast walk, we had sent our friend Andy ahead of us purely and simply to check the truthfulness of a sign promising a bull in a field. Luckily for him, the sign had been lying.

Anyway, my wife occasionally has concerns that something will happen to me while I am out walking alone. Perhaps I will trip and break an ankle or a leg, she has suggested, or even worse, suddenly develop appendicitis. She also mentioned several more possible things that could go wrong. In fact, thinking about it, it was an alarmingly large number, which quite frankly started to make me worry. Perhaps she was planning something?

Anyway, I am not sure how useful being with someone else would be if you had a heart attack at the top of a mountain. I certainly wouldn't be much good to anyone else, as even though I have done more first aid courses than I care to remember, I don't think I would be able to do a triple heart bypass at the top of Ben Nevis or remove Rob's appendix if a real emergency did occur.

I could comfort you and tell you that everything would be okay, but in all honesty, I would probably be crossing my fingers behind my back, and I might well be lying, come to think of it. At a push, I could probably call the emergency services, but again, I am not sure how useful that would be in the long term.

Anyway, we both concluded that there probably were some instances where being with someone else could be useful, although today's walk, which was going to be along well-worn paths in good conditions, did not seem to pose any problems.

With that, Rob fell over. You could not make this up, and I am completely honest when I say this, as it is with some irony that he did so just after discussing safety while out walking.

At the bottom of the ravine, where a bridge crossed the river, Rob had wandered over to the other side to go and check out the waterfall, while I had ventured a little further up the riverbank before crossing to get a picture of it from a distance. Belle, in her typical fashion, had followed Rob.

Picture in hand, I then crossed the bridge myself and joined Rob and Belle on the other side, and just as I approached him through the trees, I heard something that was a cross between a thud, a splash, and a girly scream.

In fact, what I heard was exactly a cross between a thud, a splash, and a girly scream, or more accurately, it was a combination of all three.

I stopped and looked through the trees, where I saw Rob wobbling erratically, and he was clearly trying not to go over again. It was then that I noticed he was standing on a moss-covered rock in the middle of a stream, and he looked rather wet. Belle was at his feet looking up at him, and I think she might have been laughing, to be honest.

I shouted to see if he was okay, but he was clearly not, and he shouted that he might have broken his wrist.

As he cleared the trees and the water, I could see that all of his right side was soaked, but more worrying than that, he was holding his right hand very close to him and almost seemed to be cuddling it. Slowly peeling his glove off, he visibly winced with pain, and once it was removed, it was clear to see that something was wrong.

A small cut leaked red stuff onto his palms, which assured me that Rob was probably at least human and not some kind of cyborg, but the main problem seemed to be the rather large lump somewhere in the vicinity of his fifth metacarpal. It was almost cartoon-like, and I had visions of Bugs Bunny looking dazed before me, which possibly puzzled Rob when I started laughing about this at the back of my mind.

He said his hand was numb, but Rob's wife had often told me he had no feelings anyway, so I did not worry too much about that.

I asked him if he could move his fingers, and as he slowly squeezed them into a clenched fist, I suggested to him that nothing was broken, and he was just a big drama king and that he should get over it.

We are like that, us men, and we fully support each other as friends and comrades, which is why I helped him by telling him to grow a pair.

After a minute or two of quite literally twiddling his fingers, he decided that he probably hadn't broken it and said that he could definitely go on after all.

Before we did move on, though, I asked him what had happened, and he said that he had been following Belle into the water to try and bring her back and that he had stood on a rather slippery rock, at which point gravity seemingly took over.

I looked him in the eye and asked him how he sleeps at night, shook my head, and muttered something about trying to blame the dog, shame on him. He tries that at home when he farts, too, and he doesn't even have a dog.

Leaving the waterfall and a rather surprisingly large trail of blood behind us, the path immediately took us upwards and away from the river. We were heading due east now, and below us, to the south, we could see the low route we had done last time disappearing off down a valley following the course of the River Swale.

It all looked very nice today, as well. The sun was as bright as ever, and there was hardly a cloud in the sky, although the ground was still frozen beneath our feet, and in some places treacherously so.

We were on the southern flank of Baldi Hill, I told Rob, before quickly correcting myself to Beldi Hill, a mistake which I explained away as momentary confusion caused by bright sunlight glinting off his big shiny head.

The path twisted this way and that, and the going was slow, as every now and then, we would find ourselves walking across black ice, which seemed as smooth as glass. Parts of the path were wetter than others, which became a problem in the shaded areas, and it looked as if this ice had settled in for the winter.

We were on the lookout for Crackpot Hall, which was somewhere not far ahead of us, although we only saw it when we were almost right upon it, being over the brow of a hill as it was until almost the last minute.

Crackpot Hall, it should be said, was never a hall. Used variously as a farm and then as offices, it is perhaps one of the most famous ruins within the Yorkshire Dales, probably partly due to its unusual name.

Perhaps the most famous story associated with the hall, though, is the tale of the feral child that was once said to have lived in the surrounding hills. Made famous by Ella Pontefract and Marie Hartley in the 1930s, who we last met at the museum in Hawes, of course, Alice is said to have been a wild-eyed and wilder-haired little thing who lived here alone, far removed from society, and who spoke a hard-to-understand dialect. She was made to sound almost witch-like and was described as having a mocking, chuckling laugh

However, all of this is not entirely true, and in fact, the story was somewhat sensationalized at the time, probably to sell newspapers. Many years later, David Almond, a BBC journalist, finally managed to get to the bottom of the real story after tracking feral Alice down. It turns out, then, that Alice was nothing like feral, but in fact, she lived here with her parents and five siblings and simply enjoyed roaming the beautiful countryside as a sort of free-range child, much like the children of Amanda Owen today, I imagine.

We had a quick mooch in the derelict buildings that littered the site, but as there was not a lot to see, and certainly nothing worth stealing, we were soon back on the track, which took us left around a bluff and down into Swinner Gill. This steep-sided dale was spectacularly beautiful at this time of the morning, and we had the whole place to ourselves. Not a sound echoed around us, and although strong winds had been forecast for today, we felt only a mild breeze.

We made our way along the edge of the hill, towards a small waterfall at the head of the dale, where we crossed a bridge that was directly above the waterfall. After another photo opportunity, and after a quick look at the map, we realized we had to carry on upwards and head directly east towards the top of the hill. Until then, we had thought we would be edging along the top of the hill to the south.

As the path got higher, it became more and more frozen, and while Rob and I took baby steps over the solid ice that we encountered every few feet, Belle was doing her usual dance around the countryside and was clearly having much fun indeed.

Unfortunately, she was having too much fun, and I witnessed this personally when I saw her eat some dog poo. I closed my eyes in disgust, but it was too late, and rather than go on a rant about people not picking up after their dogs, I went into denial instead.

Apparently, dogs do this for a reason. It can often be due to an enzyme deficiency, which can be quite common in dogs fed solely on processed dried foods. This act even has a name, coprophagia, which sounds almost as disgusting as the act itself. Of course, dogs are not alone in this but are joined by many other creatures in the natural world. Mice have been known to exhibit this same behaviour, but the king of coprophagia has to be the humble guinea pig. They are notorious for doing this, apparently, and have been recorded reusing their own poo up to fifty times in an hour. Think about that the next time you see one of those fluffy little cuties.

In their defence, though, dogs will generally only eat fresh poo, and when I say fresh, I mean less than two days old. They don't eat poo older than that because that would just be disgusting, wouldn't it?

The climb up was incredibly tiring, and I found myself having to stop every now and then to have a rest. Looking back, I was rewarded with magnificent views back down Swinner Gill deep into the dale below, spoilt only by the image of an old bald man huffing and puffing his way behind me. In fairness, though, the only difference was the hair, as I was huffing and puffing too, and come to think of it, I don't have that much hair left either. Still, it's good to poke fun at one's friends, don't you think, especially when they are big, old and bald.

What we were actually looking at on the hillside to the south was the site and remains of one of the most productive lead mines that this area ever saw, and this was Adelaide Level Mine. The mine is named after Adelaide Denys, the daughter of Sir George Denys, one-time owner of Draycott Manor in nearby Fremington. Sir George also owned much of Swaledale in his time and was heavily involved in mining, particularly lead, which is where he made the bulk of his fortune and is why he named his most successful mine after his daughter.

The bulk of the fortune came in 1865 when £12,000 worth

of lead ore was discovered here, and while that may still be a lot of money now, back then, it was an absolute fortune equivalent to many millions of pounds. More modest discoveries continued on a regular basis, with another large bounty found in 1918, but shortly after that, the mine flooded and was abandoned. It was actually lost and buried until being rediscovered in 1998, and the entrance has since been restored. The keystone on the mine, which is engraved with Adelaide Level AD 1867, is actually a replica, with the original now being held in the Swaledale Museum in Reeth, and the ruined building that can still be seen here is actually the old mine shop, although I wouldn't have thought they would have much in stock today.

Unfortunately, Adelaide was not quite as successful in life as the mine that bore her name, and she married a cad by the name of Sir James Lamont, who somehow became an MP but who then spent most of his time exploring the arctic and bashing seal's heads in. It appears that the apple doesn't fall far from the tree, as their first-born son Alexander also went off looking for adventure, but he ended up being shot and killed in the Boer War, and their second son Norman somehow managing to get himself gored to death by a bull in Trinidad. I never even knew they had bulls in Trinidad.

Before we leave the mine and Adelaide behind once and for all, I'm going to go on a bit of a tangent now, as I often do, but it will be worth it, I promise. Adelaide Denys, you see, was also the descendant of a man called George Jeffreys, an English aristocrat who lived during the 1600s, who never went to America, but is now nonetheless probably at least partly buried in Fulton, Missouri, in the United States, sort of. Let me explain.

While we may not have heard of Jeffreys by name, he entered our history as the Hanging Judge. What this means is that he was the yes man to King James II, and it was, therefore, Jeffreys that sent many men to their deaths on behalf of the king. However, this became a bit of a problem when the king fled the country in the Glorious Revolution of 1688. Jeffreys was soon arrested in a pub in London while trying to flee, disguised, not very well by all accounts, as a sailor. He was actually recognized by someone who had somehow managed to survive his harsh justice. Once his identity was clear, he was immediately arrested, and finally, he was thrown in the Tower of London, which is where he ultimately died. That really should be the end of his story, but it isn't.

After his death, you see, his friends lobbied for and were granted permission to move his remains to St Mary's Church in Aldermanbury in central London, which is where he should have remained forever. However, perhaps not for the first time in this book, Hitler intervened, and his Luftwaffe pilots managed to bomb the church to kingdom come during the blitz of 1940.

Rather than rebuild the church, the rubble was left in a pile until 1966, when it was loaded up and sold to some enterprising Americans, who sorted through it all and rebuilt the church as a memorial to Winston Churchill on the grounds of Fulton University. It is in Fulton, Missouri, you see, where Churchill gave one of the most famous speeches of his life in 1946 when he warned of the Russian Menace and of the Iron Curtain that was about to descend across all of Europe, and which perhaps explains why they wanted a church from London in the first place. Anyway, it is not unfeasible to think that some bits of Jeffreys were among the rubble, so there you go.

I had noticed Rob begin to yawn at all of this history, so we moved on with our walk. After what seemed an age, the gradient settled out a little and became less intense, and we also joined what could be described as a track rather than the treacherous path that we had just dragged ourselves up.

The track was as wide as a vehicle, and in fact, more specifically, we decided it was as wide as a tractor when we stumbled across a big blue one a short while later. There was no one around, though, so we figured that it had just been left up here, as it was maybe a difficult job getting it up and down the mountain every time the farmer wanted to do some farming stuff.

We passed some grouse butts and shooting boxes as we crossed the plateau, with never-ending views all around once again giving us that on top of the world feeling. Odd patches of ice still threatened to take us down, but all in all, this part of the walk was both easy and pleasant.

Easy and pleasant apart from the deranged things with feathers that again decided to come charging out of the heather every now and then, breaking both the silence and my patience. Why are these things so loud anyway? Is it a defence mechanism designed to frighten away predators? If so, then surely these grouse and pheasants could just take one look at Rob and me, at which point they would quickly realize that we are not predators at all. In fact, they would probably feel sorry for us and promptly serve themselves up on a plate, all nicely plucked and cooked.

We walked on and soon passed a hill called Rogan's Seat to our left. For whatever reason, this hill has become somewhat famous for being the most boring hill in Yorkshire, which seemed just a tad unfair, to be honest. Some even go further and call it the most boring in the whole country, which quite frankly beggars belief. I can knock this accusation clearly out of the park right now because on the north-western slope of Rogan's Seat is the highest pub in Britain, the Tan Hill Inn, and no other hill or mountain can claim that, can they? If you remember, I had mentioned that the pub was cut off for a while, way back in 2010. Well, I can now update you and let you know that it was cut off again at the end of 2021, at more or less exactly the same time as Rob, Belle and myself had been trudging through the snow a few weeks ago, which hopefully confirms that I really wasn't exaggerating about the cold weather.

While we are up here, now might be a good time to highlight the difference between a hill, a fell and a seat. Allow me to explain.

In old Norse, hvall or holl meant something like an isolated or rounded hill. It is not surprising, then, to find out that Norse Vikings settled these dales over a thousand years ago, which ultimately explains why several peaks around here became hills.

Seat, again from an old Norse word, this time saeti, is usually used in the names of lofty hills, and these are often preceded with the name of the local Lord, such as Hugh Seat and Simon's Seat.

And as for fell, it is from yet another old Norse word, fiall, which was used for the highest and most prominent hills, which we would now usually call mountains. This is perhaps why the use of fell is quite common in the Lake District, whereas round here, it is used solely for Great Shunner Fell, the highest mountain in these hills and, of course, the third-highest in Yorkshire.

So there you go, the names are all down to the Vikings, particularly the Norse Vikings, and they serve to give us a clue about the shape and height of the hills.

My thoughts turned to food, so I suggested to Rob that we stop at the next available opportunity, something that he agreed with wholeheartedly. A quick look at the map suggested Gunnerside Gill, just a mile or so ahead of us. There appeared to be some disused buildings that would hopefully provide a nice enough picnic spot. With this in mind, we plodded on.

It wasn't long before we slowly found ourselves going downhill, and after briefly missing a turn off for our path because we were busy talking, we were soon heading down very steep slopes indeed through a landscape that appeared to be more rubbish dump than anything else.

The path twisted and turned, and despite one or two slippery incidents, we somehow managed not to fall to our deaths but ended up on the slopes of Gunnerside Gill itself.

We had great views to both the north and south, though we were heading north, and sure enough, there was a small collection of old buildings which looked like a most excellent place to stop.

As we descended into the dale along a switchback of a path, we did see another couple far below us, and while I saw Rob wave to them, I did not see them wave back.

I caught him up at the bottom, which of course meant I also caught Belle up as she had been stuck to him like glue, and a hundred yards later, we found ourselves choosing our picnic spot, of which there were many fine choices.

We settled on a low wall that was both in the sun and shielded from the wind by a higher wall behind. I was pretty hungry by now, but as usual, I fed Belle first, which meant one thing. By the time I started eating, she had finished her lunch and now wanted mine.

Rob poured us a coffee, and we sat and discussed what each building had probably been, though some were completely beyond recognition after years of decay, so we were probably completely wrong.

After finishing his sandwiches, Rob pulled a banana out of his lunchbox, and I told him I had an interesting fact to share with him about such fruits. He pre-empted me and told me he knew they were radioactive, but that was not the fact I was going to share, and mine was better; in fact, it was far better.

Bananas, you see, produce anti-matter. It's true, they really do, and it is all to do with something called potassium-40. This is a very specific and incredibly rare form of potassium that occurs naturally among more normal potassiums, but only to the tune of only around 100 parts per million. And it is this special potassium that does indeed produce a positron of anti-matter every now and then.

Now, bearing in mind that bananas contain lots and lots of lovely potassium, the normal kind of course, hence the often-told story that they are radioactive, it stands to reason that a tiny fraction of this is, therefore, potassium-40, and therefore it also stands to reason that your average humble banana is popping out a positron of anti-matter every now and then.

I'm not an expert on maths, so I have left it to the nerds to do the sums, but apparently, this still means that your humble banana will indeed pop out a positron of anti-matter about once every seventy-five minutes or so. And they say bananas are good for you.

While we were eating, a young couple passed, but they did not say hello and looked to be far too into each other, so the cynic inside of me suggested that they had not known each other all that long. Rob agreed and added that they might also be married, though not to each other, which made me laugh.

I flew my drone here just to get a couple of quick pictures of the buildings, but I must mention that Belle does not like drones. She has often barked at it, but apparently, today, her tactic was to try and pee on it before it took off, which, let's face it, could have been quite painful for her.

I have heard of dogs peeing on all sorts of things over the years, but for me, the best story I have come across is that of Juliana. Juliana was a Great Dane, and when I say great, I really do mean great. Her story occurred at the height of the Second World War when bombs were falling left, right and centre all over the country. Unfortunately for Juliana, her home was one of those hit by a bomb, though luckily, it was an incendiary bomb, so it did not explode as such.

Juliana must have heard the commotion of the bomb crashing through the roof of the house and, as dogs do, immediately went to investigate. Seeing the smoking bomb burning away on the rug in front of the fire, Juliana did the only thing she could do, and she peed on it. She must have had a fair amount to drink, as she managed to completely put the thing out, became briefly famous as a result, and was awarded a Blue Cross medal for her bravery.

That wasn't the end of her heroics, though. Towards the end of the war, Juliana discovered the family home on fire one night. This fire was just a bit too big to pee on, though, so instead, she woke everyone up and saved their lives, though unfortunately, the house was still destroyed. Juliana was given yet another medal for her troubles, though I think she would have definitely preferred a nice juicy bone.

Incidentally, the Blue Cross Society, which began life as the rather rudely named Our Dumb Friends League in 1897, was closed in 1951. However, the medals were reinstated in 2006 to honour a police explosives sniffer dog called Jake, who helped clear tube lines in London after the 7/7 bombings. Who knew?

Lunch was soon over, which meant one thing and one thing only; we had to head uphill again. The path continued straight up the hill to our east, onto the tops of Gunnerside Moor. I had one more story to tell Rob, which I did while we walked, and it was one that I promised Rob he would be interested in, as will you, I imagine. This one concerns Gunnerside Moor, which was basically much of the landscape that was currently all around us. I do apologize for going off on a tangent now, and I am the first to admit that this one is a huge tangent, but it is interesting, I promise, and well, one thing simply led to another.

As we found ourselves heading east across Gunnerside Moor then, we were actually crossing possibly the finest grouse moor in the country, and it is in fact considered to be the holy grail when it comes to shooting noisy things with feathers, apparently. Every year on the Glorious Twelfth, an incredibly select few are invited to come up here and blast this way and that on this 32,000-acre estate, which belongs to someone called Robert Miller. He might have an ordinary name, but Miller is, in fact, an American billionaire who has done rather well for himself. He is also a record-breaking sailor holding a couple of transatlantic records, which is no mean feat, and on top of this, his daughter married into the Greek royal family, making her none other than the Crown Princess of Greece.

Anyway, Miller is currently doing an excellent job of looking after this place, as I discover when yet another startled grouse chatters out from the foliage and barks past my head in alarm. I'm not sure if the grouse was trying to give me a heart attack deliberately or if it was just really lucky, but there you go.

Even poor Belle almost jumped out of her skin, and normally she would be off and chasing such a tasty snack, but as I looked down at her, she simply cowered behind me with her tail between her legs. Perhaps she was just startled by the grouse, or perhaps she knew that this area is supposed to be haunted by a figure of a lady in a black dress that died in a fire many years ago. Regardless, I called her a chicken, and we moved on.

As well as being a good place to grab dinner, then, there is also an amazing chunk of history that links this place to the wider world, and when I say the wider world, I mean events involving saboteurs and spies and assassins and all that stuff. Bear with me on this, please, as it might take a while to get there, but like I said, it will be worth it.

The story starts in the dark days of the Second World War, when Britain was fighting alone and while much of Europe had fallen to the Nazis, with America yet to join the party. At that time, the Gunnerside Estate was owned by a man called Charles Hambro, a wealthy investment banker born in 1897 who had already seen some action in the First World War and who wanted to do something in the second. Indeed, he had been awarded the Military Cross in 1917 when he had ventured across a canal into enemy territory to rescue two of his comrades and then later the same day led a charge with nothing but a revolver. Through this bravery, he somehow managed to account for four heavily armed enemy troops, so it is important not to merely think of him as a banker.

Fast forward to the Second World War, then, and it could be said that Hambro had a personal interest in what was going on. He was of Jewish heritage, and his ancestors' beloved home of

Denmark was now firmly under Nazi control. Charles had been working for the family business in the inter-war years, Hambro's Bank, which itself had often been linked to the murky world of espionage, so it did not take long for him to become involved in the fun and shenanigans that was to make his war unique to that of any other.

He initially became involved in work in Scandinavia, arranging the smuggling of both people and weapons in both directions, building intelligence networks and, of course, blowing stuff up. It was the latter that was to become his favourite, as we will find out as the story goes along.

Being rather talented in his field, then, it wasn't long before Hambro was asked to join the Ministry of Economic Warfare, which was, of course, a cover name for the people that ran secret agents at the time, which was really the Special Operations Executive, or SOE for short. Quite amusingly, they became much better known, at least among those in the know, by their nickname, the Ministry of Ungentlemanly Warfare, and were the obvious people to go to when something extremely sensitive came about or when you wanted to blow stuff up, which is exactly what came next.

The allies, you see, had become aware that the Nazis were trying to develop an atomic bomb, and one element essential to the making of that bomb was something called heavy water. At the time, there was only one place in the world that made heavy water, and that was at the Vermork hydroelectric power plant in the Telemark region of southern Norway. Heavy water was important because it was needed in order to breed plutonium, which was the actual fissile material of the bomb. The only alternative to breeding plutonium would be to go and dig up lots of Uranium, which was clearly not possible during wartime, at least not for the Nazis.

Hambro, then, devised two missions that were intended to destroy the plant along with any heavy water they found, a plan which, if it succeeded, would make it impossible for the Nazis to develop nuclear weapons. Recalling his love of shooting on his lands up here, Hambro named the first mission Operation Grouse, which saw four agents dropped into the occupied territory around the power station to prepare the groundwork, and among them was a young man called Knut Haugland. Operation Freshman came next, which was the actual mission to blow stuff up, but unfortunately, this failed before it had even begun, with most of the troops involved being either injured, killed or captured when both of their gliders crashed into the frozen mountains of Norway.

Hambro went back to the drawing board and came back up here to the north of England, where he began planning what he called Operation Gunnerside, taking its name from the village and the fell, of course. The troops who were going to be sent on this mission were then trained up here, right in the middle of these moors, in the bitterly cold January of 1943, something which should have given them at least a taste of Norway I can assure you, and by February, they were ready to go.

This time, the troops were dropped by parachute so as to avoid any further unfortunate incidents with gliders, and their equipment was also dropped by parachute a few days later. Unfortunately for them, however, a Norwegian civilian found one of the crates and decided to bury it, although with the wholly good intention of not wanting it to fall into Nazi hands.

Anyway, the operation went ahead on the night of 27th February 1943, led by 23-year-old Joachim Ronneberg. Unfortunately, however, the Nazis had been alerted by the earlier failed attempt of Operation Grouse, which meant that there were now 3,000 troops defending the power station and the secrets that it contained.

This was a huge problem, as Operation Gunnerside consisted of just a handful of men, though luckily, one of them was a young man called Leif Tronstad. Tronstad was the actual designer of the heavy water production facility at Vemork, so he knew it like the back of his hand. Furthermore, he actually came up with large parts of the plan to blow the thing sky high.

Before we go on, we should remind ourselves that these men all had normal jobs before the war and were, therefore, simply ordinary men doing extraordinary things. Indeed, their ranks included a tour guide, a teacher, a postman and a factory worker, among others.

To counter the high number of guards, then, they first had to climb down a frozen ravine, cross a treacherous icy river and scale the cliffs at the other side. Despite the odds, they were somehow successful, and the only person the saboteurs came across in the power station was the caretaker, a man named Johansen.

While all was good so far, Johansen did manage to lose his spectacles which, quite bizarrely, almost derailed the whole operation. This maybe makes more sense when we remind ourselves that new glasses were not only incredibly hard to come by but were also very expensive during the war years and were thus prized possessions, but still, we should perhaps remember that those horrible Nazis were trying to build a nuclear bomb.

Anyway, luckily, the glasses were eventually found, and in the early hours of 28th February, someone somewhere pressed a detonator which, unfortunately, woke up every single one of those nasty Nazi troops that had been sent here to protect the place, with the early morning wake-up call presumably making each and every one of them somewhat pissed off. However, none was probably more so than the Nazi commander up here, a formidable man called General Folkenhorst, although he later described the military operation against him as a brilliant coup, which is high praise indeed and a clear testament to the success of the mission.

And although the 3,000 Nazi troops did their best to catch the saboteurs, the whole Gunnerside team did all eventually manage to escape, which meant they also lived to fight another day.

Knut Haugland survived the war and had a particularly interesting adventure when he ended up on Thor Heyerdahl's Kon-Tiki Expedition in 1947, which aimed to prove that the South Sea Islands of the Pacific had originally been populated by people sailing from Peru. Heyerdahl, Haugland and four others set sail on a boat constructed using only materials and techniques that would have been possible to use centuries before.

Inevitably, Haugland finally passed away on Christmas Day, although this was much later in 2009, when he was 92, and after he had lived a most interesting and satisfying life. Lastly, it is interesting to note that Haugland had originally met Heyerdahl at a special forces training camp during the war and that Thor Heyerdahl was, therefore, probably a spook as well.

Leif Tronstad was sadly killed in the last days of the war defending his homeland, but Joachim Ronneberg survived the war and lived the longest of the lot, passing away peacefully aged 92 in 2018 after a long and happy life.

General Falkenhorst, on the other hand, was arrested at the war's end and tried for war crimes. Initially sentenced to death, this was commuted to 20-years imprisonment, but he was released in 1953 on the grounds of ill health, though he still managed to cheekily last another fifteen years, passing away quietly while at home in 1968.

As for Charles Hambro, he left SOE and went to work in Washington, rather appropriately working as a liaison officer on the program that eventually produced the atomic bombs dropped on Japan, which finally ended the war in late 1945. He lived on after the war, once again pursuing a career in banking, which must have been something of a come-down, you would expect, and he, too, passed away peacefully, at home in 1963 after a happy and fulfilling life, though he was only a relatively young 65-years-old.

If any of this sounds vaguely or even very familiar, then you may have seen the 1965 movie *The Heroes of Telemark*, which tells of this story in great detail and stars handsome chisel-chinned actor Kirk Douglas. However, some of those involved in these events were not entirely happy with the film's many alleged inaccuracies, so when Ray Mears filmed his documentary *The Real Heroes of Telemark* in 2003, many took the chance to set the record straight, particularly Knut Haugland. Regardless, it all started up here, right in the heart of Gunnerside Moor. Bet you never knew that?

And before we leave this subject completely, we should remember the Norwegian patriot who had safely hidden away one of the supply containers for Operation Gunnerside. He later stumbled across a team of British Army soldiers conducting arctic warfare training in the area in 1976, which was, of course, some thirty years after the end of the war. When he met them, he told them about the container he had found so long before, took them to it and even helped them dig it up. It was later returned to the United Kingdom and has since been on display at the Imperial War Museum.

I think Rob found this story interesting, but as we had been talking all about it, we realized we had failed to notice the bizarre landscape that was all around us. To say it was a wasteland would be an understatement, and piles of spoil littered the landscape as far as the eye could see.

It was up here that we bumped into a couple of people who turned out to be the two we had seen when making our way down into Gunnerside Gill just before lunch. They had waved back, apparently, and we had a short but friendly conversation about the usual things before they dropped back and let us go on ahead of them.

We actually left them as we passed the ruins of an old ore crushing machine which had been rotting away up here for decades and which has become quite famous locally. It was still remarkably solid despite years of neglect, and its bright colours contrasted nicely with the faded pastels of the moonscape within which it stood.

This landscape continued for quite some time, and I mentioned to Rob that if we had come this way when it had been covered in snow, it would have been an incredibly challenging route, given the featureless nature of the path. Because waste from the mines had been dumped all over this area, you could, in theory, walk over most of it, and you would still have the feeling of a gravel track beneath your feet, so a covering of snow would make following the actual path very difficult indeed, if not completely impossible.

On a positive note, however, Belle had the freedom to run wherever she wanted at this stage, though I did wonder if the stones would eventually begin to hurt her feet. However, there was no sign of that at the moment as she galloped this way and that, absolutely in her element, apparently.

As the path took a decidedly downward tone, we were approaching our next stop, the disused Old Gang Mine, which I had seen pictures of many times but had never visited. It is a large complex of everything needed to run a Victorian mine, and on paper, it looked impressive, though, in person, it was even more so.

The first building we saw was a simple hut, but we could see a whole host of derelict buildings in the distance, some of which were quite substantial. There was also an interesting looking tunnel just across from the hut, so we dropped our backpacks and went to investigate. I grabbed my torch and jumped down into the stream that bubbled out of the tunnel, and hopped from rock to rock into the inky darkness as far as I could go.

Rob followed me, and although we were soon as far in as we could go without getting incredibly wet, the torch lit up at least fifty yards more, which disappeared around a mysterious bend. I wished I had brought some waterproof boots so I could continue, but as we still had a few miles to go today and because I had my new shoes on, there was no way I was going any further.

We sat on a bench outside the hut, enjoying both the sunshine and the rest of our food. Belle hovered between the two of us, picking up every crumb that we managed to drop, and Rob found a pack of spicy chicken in the bottom of his bag that he had brought specifically for Belle.

He laughed and told me that he wasn't going to be responsible for what might happen in a few hours, as the chicken was, in fact, really spicy, but I chuckled when I remembered that we were in his car.

It was quite breezy on our little bench, but the early afternoon sun kept us surprisingly warm considering the time of year and also that this whole area had been covered in deep snow just a couple of weeks earlier.

Finishing our lunch, we tried to have a look in the hut, which was unfortunately locked, though Rob found an open shutter that at least allowed us to peer in through a locked window. The inside was sparse but would undoubtedly be very much welcomed in the middle of a storm.

We moved on and had a look at the various other buildings, which included a rather tall chimney. Rob commented that this complex would have been considered both state of the art and huge in its day and would have brought much money into the local economy. He was probably right, but it was still tiny when you think of today's factories.

We moved on, leaving the ruins of Old Gang Mine behind us, and the path snaked along roughly following the course of a rock-strewn stream. We only met one person, and Rob asked him if we were going the right way for London, and worryingly, the gentleman said that yes, we were.

The path spat us out at Surrender Bridge, where we did not actually cross the bridge but did cross a small road, looking for yet another old smelting mill, but we must have taken a wrong turn, as we ended up high above it.

Interestingly, there is a common misconception that Surrender Bridge was the site of one battle or another and thus marks the location of a military capitulation, but this is all tosh, and the truth is both much simpler and incredibly disappointing, I am afraid. The bridge, you see, is actually named after the moors above, namely Surrender Moor or alternatively Surrender Moss, a bleak but peaty hillside where people once gathered peat turves for fuel in the days before coal was available, which is what the Moss part of the name denotes.

Anyway, being the lazy sort that we are, we decided not to go back down the hill as it looked as if the path that we were on rejoined the route anyway a little bit further on. And indeed it did, but again, we took another wrong turn, this one more serious, and somewhat perplexingly, we now ended up too far down the hill instead.

However, it did not take us long to get on the right track, and once I had the map the right way up, we followed a muddy path that skirted around Calver Hill. Belle was once again sploshing through huge puddles, although she struggled on those that were still frozen. She walked across one that seemingly offered a solidly frozen surface despite my warnings not to, so I was not surprised when she went straight through the ice into a few inches of water. I chuckled at her misfortune, but in fairness, she was now much cleaner than she had been.

We followed the path along dry stone walls to our right, deep in conversation, which once again meant that we took yet another wrong turn just before Healaugh. Luckily, a quick backtrack soon had us back on the right path and heading down to Barney beck, a small mountain stream that was, in fact, the same one that had passed Old Gang Mine but which now had a different name.

This path was much better to walk on, especially for Belle, and offered a thick carpet of turf beneath her feet, although it was quite steep. This was not a problem for her, though, as she still ran this way and that, and at one point, she once again rolled in something rather nasty. At least she hadn't eaten it, I thought.

At the bottom of this hill, I heard a little girl scream ahead of me and realized that Rob had once again almost gone over. He had pushed that hard on his walking pole, he said, that it had shortened by around six inches.

Through the gate and onto a track that would take us into Healaugh village itself, we stopped momentarily to examine what looked to me like a small piece of rope. Rob wondered if it was a dead snake, but upon closer examination, it actually turned out to be a slow worm.

Paradoxically, a slow worm is neither a snake nor a worm but is actually a legless lizard and is probably the most unusual lizard in Britain. They are interesting in that they have a couple of ingenious methods of defending themselves. Firstly, if they feel threatened, they might consider pooing at or on their attacker, so pick one up at your own peril. Secondly, if someone or something grabs hold of them, they can detach their tail, which is usually just enough to distract whatever predator is eyeing them up for lunch.

If you ever see something like this, the best way to confirm it is a slow worm is to look at its eyes. If it blinks, it's a slow worm, as snakes don't have eyelids. And they are amazing in that they can live for up to twenty years, sometimes even longer.

This one might not have been dead as such, as it may have just been the remnants of one that had shed its skin, which they do in sections. To be honest, if you saw one, you would probably just assume it to be a snake, but anyway, you should consider yourself very lucky indeed if you do ever come across one in the wild, regardless of whether it is a snake or a lizard, come to think of it.

We followed the path into Healaugh, where we stopped momentarily at the benches at the far end of the village. There was nothing to do here and nothing to see, but we stopped anyway as we wanted to take a photo of ourselves on one of the benches.

We had passed here while doing the Coast-to-Coast walk a few years before, after having walked the low route from Reeth, and we had been lucky in that some friends of ours met us here. Even luckier, they had brought a cake, and a good friend of ours who had been walking with us and who was also called Rob had claimed two pieces of cake when everyone else had one. It's silly what you can remember from years ago, but anyway, we had a chuckle about this, took a photo, admittedly without any cake in sight, and sent it to the other Rob anyway.

From here, we were back in the fields, and once again, there were sheep hanging about here and there. Belle had been lucky in that she had spent much of the day running free, so she did not seem too happy about being back on her lead, although we were only a mile or two from Reeth, so she would not be on it for long.

We skipped from field to field through those horrible narrow gates, accompanied by an even narrower squeeze at each one, and despite yet another wrong turn which caused us to have to scale a sheer cliff face at some point, we soon had Reeth in our sights.

Ironically, and perhaps as should be expected by now, this was the muddiest section of the walk, though thankfully, some of it was once again beginning to freeze over. Belle managed to find a puddle, though, and had a drink of something similar to hot chocolate, much to my disgust, although she certainly seemed to enjoy it.

Just before we walked into Reeth, we spotted a lone kestrel hovering in the sky above. Its body was almost quivering, which reminded me of something my uncle had told me many years before, something which I had tremendous trouble believing at the time. If you remember that hedgehogs were not always called hedgehogs and used to be called urchins, Kestrels have not always been known by their modern name. I'm not even going to ask you to guess what their old name was, as it is that ridiculous, and I don't think anyone would get it in a thousand years. Kestrels, you see, and I do apologize for this, but there is no other way to tell it other than how it is, used to be called wind fuckers. I kid you not.

Back in the 1600s, this is what we all would have shouted if we had seen one, and it wasn't even rude at the time. And before someone tells me that in old English, the letter F was sometimes pronounced as the letter S, well, that rule does not apply in this instance, and they really did pronounce it as the F-word.

And while the F-word did mean to copulate, it was not considered a swear word at the time, although it certainly wasn't what you would call genteel language either.

So why use this word to describe a most beautiful creature such as a kestrel? Well, if you have ever seen a kestrel hover, then you might understand. When they hover, you see, their body movements, which they are constantly adjusting so as to keep in the same place, mean they move up and down in a manner that suggests something rather rude. So, there you go. Bet you never knew that?

And while we are on the subject, why don't we gloss over some more examples of our crazy ancestors giving names to things that were not perhaps all that appropriate? For starters, there's the pinus rigida, which is not what you expect at all unless you are expecting a sturdy pine tree. What about the turdus migratorius, which is, in fact, a robin, or even the fartulum, which is a tiny snail. Lastly, another favourite of mine, the wonderfully named bugeranus, brings all sorts of things to mind, but is, in fact, nothing more than a wattled crane commonly found across parts of Africa. Fuckwind doesn't sound so bad now, does it?

We walked into the village and cut through a small housing estate, and I promised Belle that we would soon be back in The Kings Arms, where she would hopefully get her meaty treat once more and be able to lounge in front of the fire.

A quick pit stop at the car to change out of our muddy shoes was all that kept us from the pub, but when we got to the door, disaster struck as we found it locked. I'm not sure who was more disappointed, Belle or us.

Anyway, we ventured next door to The Black Bull and thankfully found it unlocked, and inside, Belle immediately found the fire.

Sprawling in front of it, presumably to dry her belly, she soon had her eyes closed, and although she didn't get a meaty treat, she was clearly more than happy, although I did hear a strange sound, and I swore I could smell spicy chicken.

AFTERWORD

Thank you for taking the time to read this book. I very much hope you enjoyed reading it as much as I enjoyed writing it. Belle and myself had a great time while doing the walking that eventually formed the backbone of this book. The fun only got better when Rob joined us, and although we completed this walk in the middle of winter, we still had a great time.

This book is part of my History Walks series of books, which can be read in any order, and which hopefully demonstrate that there is lots of history out there and all we have to do is go and look for it.

If you have any comments about my work, then please feel free to contact me anytime, with the best way being through my website at paulamess.co.uk. All feedback is very much appreciated and any mistakes are purely mine!

Thank you once again.

Now get out there and walk!